Collins

Science Expert 1

Authors
Meenakshi Atal
Debahuti Das

Preface

Collins Science Expert is a series of 14 coursebooks for Classes 1 to 8. The coursebooks for grades 1 and 2 are aligned with Environmental Studies (EVS) and grades 3 to 5 with Science. For Classes 6 to 8, there are separate coursebooks for Physics, Chemistry and Biology. This series, which is the revised edition of *Science Panorama*, is based on the **latest curriculum** prescribed by the **Council for the Indian School Certificate Examinations** and adheres to the guidelines of the National Education Policy (NEP) 2020.

In line with the curriculum, a thematic, coherent and structured approach has been followed and all new topics suggested in the curriculum have been included. The series also caters to the three domains of learning—**cognitive** (*intellectual nature*), **affective** (*attitudinal nature*) and **psychomotor** (*actionable nature*).

Aimed to answer a learner's cry: '*Teach me the way I want to learn*', this series adopts a method—**visual**, **auditory**, **kinesthetic** and **tactile** (**VAKT**)—that caters to all kinds of learners. Keeping in mind the saying 'I hear – I forget, I see – I understand and I do – I remember', a lot of hands-on activities have been incorporated. This would enable learners to understand and learn scientific concepts through experiential learning.

This series also emphasizes on developing *scientific skills* such as **observation**, **data collection**, **investigation**, **estimation**, **prediction**, **analysis** and **drawing inferences**. This would help in developing a scientific temperament in learners from a young age. The series also draws a connection between cause and effect; and focuses on the application of concepts in real-life situations. The language used is child-friendly and age-appropriate. Sufficient examples from everyday life have been given to help learners understand the concepts. A lot of colourful illustrations and well-labelled diagrams have been included to engage learners and aid in their understanding.

We would like to take this opportunity to thank all the teachers who reviewed the books and provided their valuable feedback, which helped in improving the quality of the content.

Any suggestions or constructive criticism from the users are welcome. We shall try to incorporate those in the future editions.

Authors

Key Features

The key features of ***Collins Science Expert*** series are completely aligned with *National Education Policy* (NEP) 2020. These meticulously designed key features, based on VAKT (visual, auditory, kinesthetic and tactile) learning style and the three domains of Bloom's Taxonomy which include **cognitive (intellectual skills)**, **affective (attitudinal nature)** and **psychomotor (actionable nature)**, can be used as learning strategies to help in the development of scientific and 21st Century Skills in students. These key features also aim to help students shift from rote-learning to competency-based learning.

Bloom's Taxonomy

Cognitive Domain

- Focuses on intellectual skills such as critical thinking, problem solving, and creating a knowledge base
- Expects learners to progress linearly, beginning at "remember" and ending at "create."

Features:

- Prior Knowledge
- Learning Objectives
- Let's Get Started
- Quick Revision
- Talk Time
- Concept Map
- Keywords
- Exercise
- Word to know
- Review Corner

Affective Domain

- Focuses on the attitudes, values, interests and appreciation of learners
- Focuses on allowing learners to understand what their own values are and how they have developed

Features:

- Greenathon
- Skill Booster
- Worksheets
- My Environment, My Responsibility!
- Happy Accidents
- Innovation: The Steppingstone
- Role of Science in Benefitting the Society

Psycho motor Domain

- Encompasses the ability of learners to physically accomplish tasks and perform movement and skills
- Expects learners to progress from using reflexes and basic movement to non-discursive communication and meaningfully expressive activity

Features:

- Do It Yourself
- Activities
- Skill Booster
- Worksheets
- My Eco Craft
- Innovation: The Steppingstone
- STEAM Worksheets

Skills and Learnings

Colour-coded tags and icons are used to easily identify the types of skills and learnings being addressed.

NEP Aligned Skills

21st Century Skills (21CS)

Learning Skills

- Critical Thinking
- Creativity and Innovation
- Collaboration
- Communication

Life Skills

- Flexibility and Adaptability
- Leadership and Responsibility
- Initiative and Self-direction
- Productivity and Accountability
- Social and Cross-cultural Interaction

Literacy Skills

- Information Literacy
- Media Literacy
- Technology Literacy

SUSTAINABLE DEVELOPMENT GOALS

Experiential Learning (EL)

Cross Curricular (CC)

Bloom's Taxonomy (BT)

Art Integration (AI)

India Focus (IF)

SEE Learning

About the Features

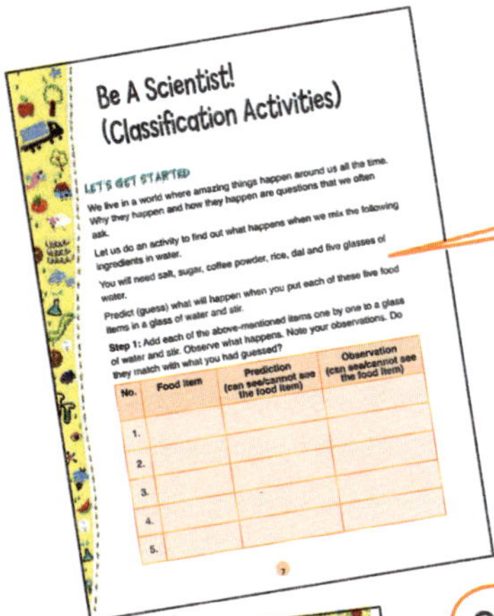

Be a Scientist! (Classes 3 to 5): Introduction to science process skills to help develop scientific attitudes

- **Concept Map:** Snapshot of the chapter in the form of a graphic organizer for quick recapitulation
- **Keywords:** Definitions of important terms

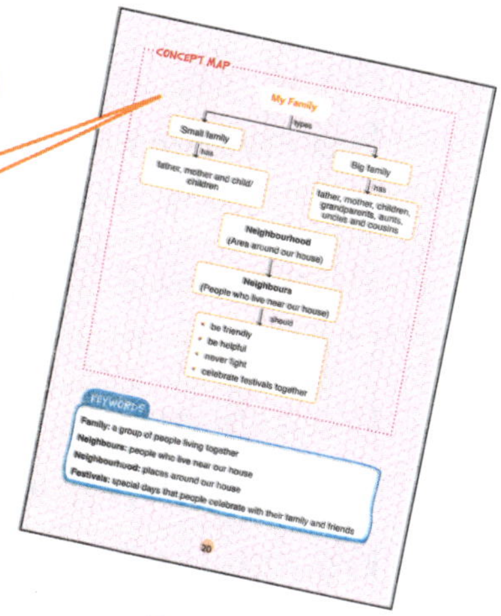

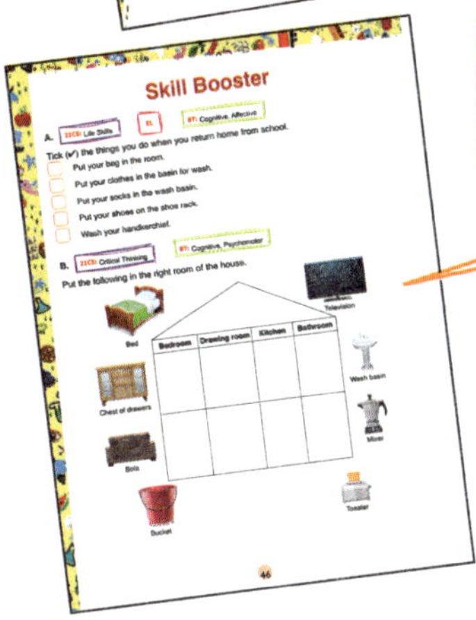

Skill Booster: Section aimed at imparting 21st Century Skills alongwith a focus on Cross-curricular Links, India Focus, Art Integration, Experiential Learning and Bloom's Taxonomy

Worksheet: Interesting questions imparting skills catering to social, emotional and ethical (SEE) needs and United Nations' sustainable development goals (SDGs)

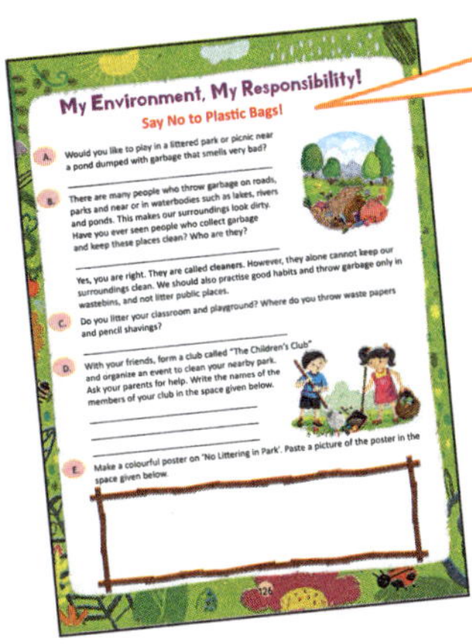

My Environment, My Responsibility! (Classes 1 and 2): Special pages to spread awareness and a sense of responsibility towards the environment

Happy Accidents (Classes 3 to 8): Interesting snippets on discoveries and inventions by chance/accidents that led to beneficial ways

STEAM Worksheets (Physics 6 to 8): Interesting project ideas integrating Science, Technology, Engineering, Arts and Mathematics to solve real-world problems

My Eco Craft (Classes 1 and 2): Hands-on activities to enhance learning beyond the classroom

Innovation: The Steppingstone (Classes 3 to 5): Ideas to guide students to solve real-life problems in innovative ways

Role of Science in Benefitting the Society (Classes 6 to 8): Snippets on the contributions made by various scientists for the development of the society

Find Out: Research-oriented questions requiring learners to look beyond the classroom

What do we call the person who treats our pet dog when it falls sick?

FIND OUT

Contents

1 About Me

Prior Knowledge

- Names of family members
- Names of some parts of body: eyes, ears and nose

Learning Objectives

- Likes and dislikes
- Hobbies
- Parts of our body
- Sense organs

LET'S GET STARTED

Me, myself!

Hello!

I am ___________.

I am a ___________ (boy/girl).

I am _______ years old.

My date of birth is ___________.

I live in ___________.

I study in ___________.

I like to ___________ ___________ ___________.

LIKES AND DISLIKES

I like ____________ colour but my friend likes ____________ colour.

I like to play____________ but my friend likes to play ____________.

HOBBIES

An activity that we enjoy doing the most in our free time is called a **hobby**. Different people have different hobbies. Reading, writing, colouring, singing and dancing are some hobbies.

Reading

Writing

Colouring

A POEM!

Do You Know Who I Am?

I am a kid, and
I am me.

I am as happy
as a kid should be!

I can sing, play
and cry.

I can be good if I try!

KNOW YOUR FRIEND BETTER!

Ask your friend the following questions.

- When is your birthday?
- Which is your favourite colour?
- What is your favourite food?
- Which is your favourite animal?
- What is your hobby?

Do you have anything in common with your friend?

PARTS OF OUR BODY

Our body has many parts. Each part has a different name and use.

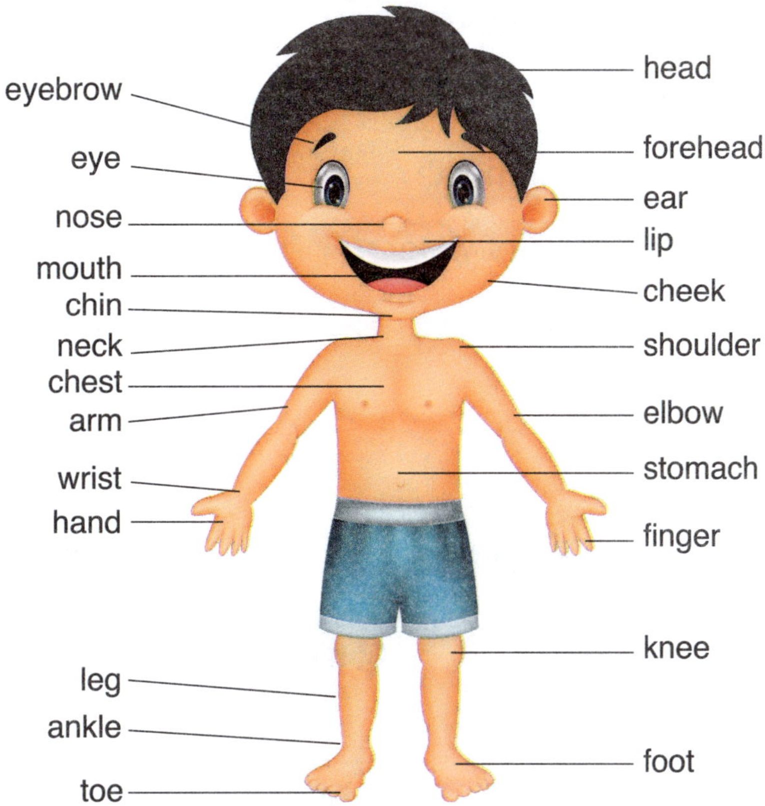

Parts of our body

Functions of Some Body Parts

The different parts of our body help us do different things.

Hands *help us write, draw and hold things.*

Mouth *helps us eat.*

Legs *help us stand, walk, run and jump.*

Shoulders *help us carry things.*

Keeping Fit

To keep ourselves fit, we should take care of our body. We should do the following to stay fit.

- Exercise and play regularly
- Eat healthy
- Drink plenty of water
- Keep our body clean

Exercise

Eating healthy

Keeping body clean

QUICK REVISION

Write T for True and F for False.

1. We cannot run with our legs.
2. We eat and sing with our mouth.
3. We should not drink a lot of water.

SENSE ORGANS

Touch, taste, hear, sight and smell are our five **senses**. Senses help us know and feel the things around us. The organs that help us sense or know about the world around us are called **sense organs**. We have five sense organs. They are eyes, ears, nose, tongue and skin.

Skin helps us touch or feel.

Tongue helps us taste our favourite food.

Ears help us hear different sounds.

Eyes help us see (sight).

Nose helps us smell.

Our five senses

TALK TIME

1. What would have happened if we had only one sense organ?
2. If you were to choose an extra sense, what would that be? Why?

CONCEPT MAP

Our Body

Uses of some body parts

- **Hands:** To write
- **Mouth:** To eat
- **Legs:** To stand, walk, run and jump
- **Shoulders:** To carry things

Sense organs

- **Eyes:** To see (sight)
- **Ears:** To hear
- **Nose:** To smell
- **Tongue:** To taste
- **Skin:** To feel (touch)

To keep fit, we must

- Exercise and play
- Eat healthy
- Drink plenty of water
- Keep clean

KEYWORDS

Parents: our mother and father

Sense organs: organs that help us know the world around us

Exercise

Objective Type Questions

A. Choose the correct answer.

1. We have ________ sense organs.
   a. three b. four c. five d. six
2. We hold things with our____________.
   a. heads b. hands c. elbows d. toes
3. To keep our body fit, we must____________.
   a. watch TV b. not play c. exercise d. not sleep
4. _______ is not a sense organ.
   a. Skin b. Ear c. Hand d. Eye
5. ________ cannot be a hobby.
   a. Reading b. Writing c. Singing d. Bathing

B. Match the following.

1. Hand 2. Foot 3. Nose 4. Head

a. 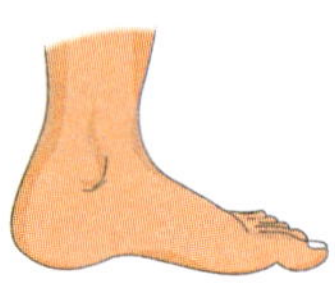
b. 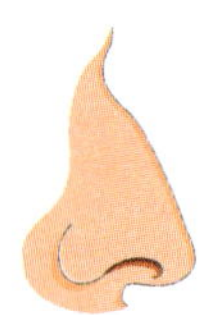
c. 
d. 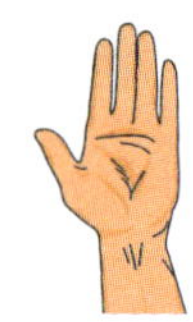

Subjective Type Questions

A. Define the following.

1. Hobbies 2. Senses 3. Sense organs

B. Answer the following questions.

1. Write any two activities that we do with the help of our hands.

   ____

2. Which part of our hand helps us hold a pencil?

   ____

3. Which part of our body helps us pedal a bicycle?

   ____

4. Name any two sense organs.

   ____

5. Which sense organ helps us identify various colours?

   ____

Application-based Question

Kritika's mother was baking a cake. While adding milk to the cake batter, her mother found that the milk had spoiled. Which sense organ did Kritika's mother use to find that the milk was spoiled? What would happen if the spoiled milk got into the cake?

Picture-based Question

Match the pictures with correct feeling words.

1. 
2. 
3. 
4. 

sad	angry	happy	surprised

Skill Booster

A. 21CS: Creativity and Innovation | AI | BT: Psychomotor

Fingerprint Tree!

You will need: Scrapbook or a craft sheet, sketch pens and watercolours.

Let us start!

1. In your scrapbook, ask an elder to draw stem and branches of a tree as shown in Fig. A.
2. Apply your favourite watercolours on your thumb.
3. Press your thumb hard on the branches of the tree to make its leaves as shown in Fig. B.
4. Your fingerprint tree is ready!

Fig. A

Fig. B

B. 21CS: Creativity and Innovation | AI | BT: Cognitive, Affective

Write your hobbies in the clouds given below and fill them with your favourite colours.

Worksheet 1

My SEE Journal

A. Do you think, Sree, Keshav and Arzoo are good friends? How?

____

____

____

____

____

____

____

____

B. What do you like to do in your free time?

____

____

____

____

My SDG Journal

11 SUSTAINABLE CITIES AND COMMUNITIES

A. Write the names of your friends.

____

____

____

____

B. Draw or paste a picture of yourself with your friends.

2 Others in My World

Prior Knowledge

- Names of different family members
- Some activities that family members do together

Learning Objectives

- Family
- My pet
- Our neighbours
- Having fun and celebrating special days

LET'S GET STARTED

Paste pictures of your family members in the frames given below.

1. My mother's name is ______________________________.
2. My father's name is _______________________________.
3. I have _____________ brothers and sisters.
4. My sister's name is ____________________.
5. My brother's name is ___________________.

FAMILY

A group of people living together who are connected to each other by birth or marriage form a **family**. Members of a family love, care and support each other. They also help each other.

A POEM!

I have a family, nice and happy,
Sharing and caring for everybody.
We like to be merry and stay healthy,
God bless my happy family!

Types of Families

There are different types of families.

A family in which a father, mother and their children live together is called a **nuclear family**. It is a small family.

A family in which grandparents, parents and their children live together is called a **joint family**. It is a large family. Sometimes, uncles, aunts and their children also live in this family.

TALK TIME

Which type of a family do you live in?

In some families, children live only with one parent, either mother or father. Such families are called **single-parent families**.

Nuclear family

Joint family

Single-parent family

Different types of families

Relationships with Family Members

Uncles, aunts, grandparents and cousins are your relatives. Your mother's and father's parents are your **grandparents**. You are their **grandchild** (**grandson** or **granddaughter**). Brothers and sisters of your parents are your **uncles** and **aunts**. Children of your uncles and aunts are your **cousins**.

Family Tree

A chart that shows the relationships between different members of a family is called a **family tree**. Let us see the family chart of Jishan.

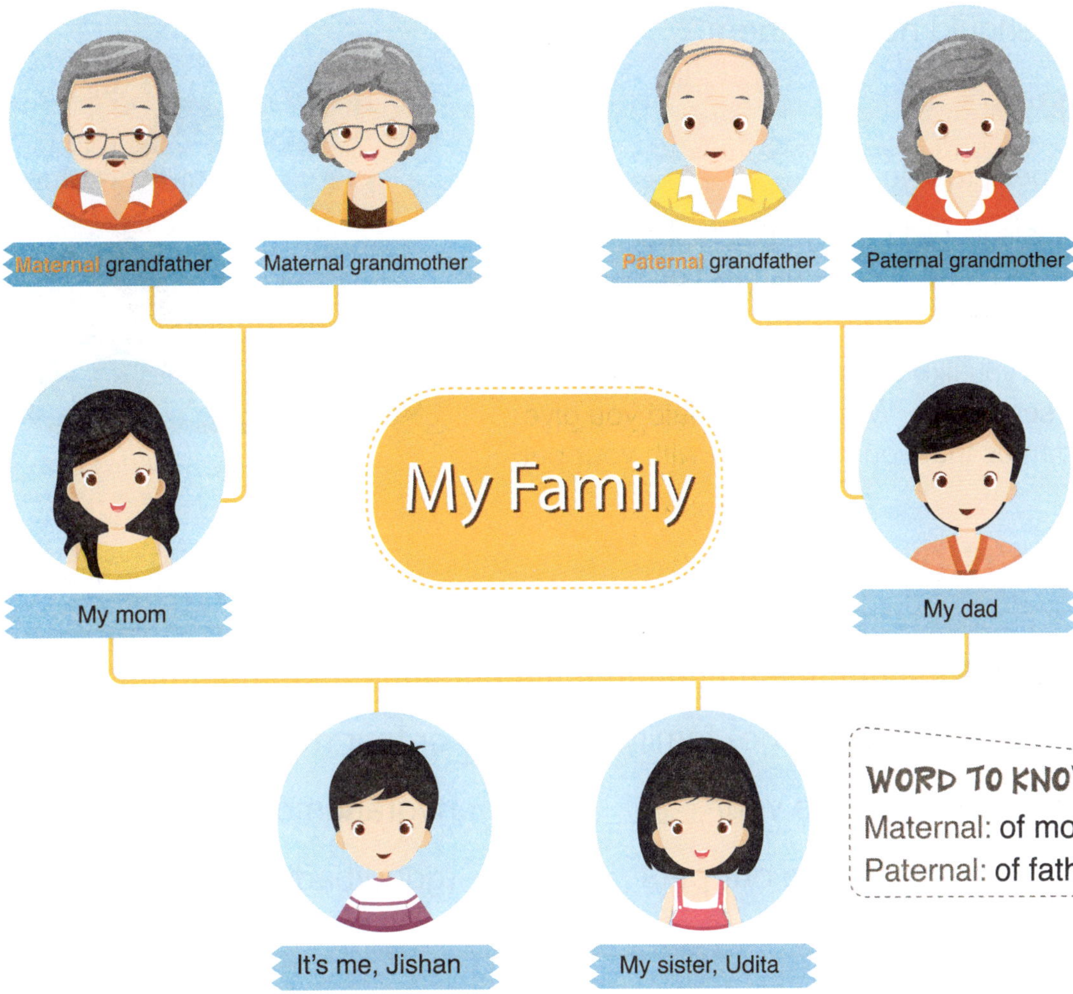

Family tree

WORD TO KNOW

Maternal: of mother's side

Paternal: of father's side

DO IT YOURSELF

Collect photographs of all your family members. Draw a family tree in your scrapbook. In the family tree, paste photographs of all your family members. Below each photo, write your relationship with the person in the picture.

Family Time!

Family members take care of each other. Parents look after their children. Siblings play and study together. We should not fight with our siblings, and we must obey our parents. Children can help their parents by setting up the table, spreading the bedsheets and by keeping their toys and books in place.

Romil helps his mother in setting the table.

MY PET

The animals that we keep and look after at home are called **pets**. Pets are a part of our family. We should give them good food and water. We should play with them. We should not hurt them.

DO IT YOURSELF

Do you have a pet? Yes/No

If so, draw or paste its picture in your scrapbook. Below its picture, write its name and the games you play with it. Show it to your teacher.

If no, what would you like to keep as a pet? Draw its picture in your scrapbook. What name would you give it? Name the games that you would play with your pet.

A girl playing with her pet

QUICK REVISION

Fill in the blanks.

1. A __________ (small/large) family has three or four members.
2. Your mother's sister is your __________ (aunt/grandmother).
3. We should always give our pets __________ (good/bad) food.

OUR NEIGHBOURS

The places around our house are our **neighbourhood**. People who live near our house are our **neighbours**. We should keep our neighbourhood clean.

Help and Respect Your Neighbours

- We should be friendly with our neighbours.
- We should help each other.
- We should celebrate festivals together.
- We should never fight with each other.

Neighbours cleaning their neighbourhood park and planting trees in it

HAVING FUN AND CELEBRATING SPECIAL DAYS

Weekends are fun times with our family and friends. We can watch television, play indoor games such as chess and ludo and outdoor games such as football, basketball and cricket or go to the neighbourhood park and have fun together.

Watching television

Playing

Ways of having fun with family and friends

TALK TIME
How do you have fun with your family?

Some days are special. We like to have fun and share our happiness with our family and friends on special days. Birthday is a special day.

Birthday celebration

Festivals are also special days. We celebrate festivals such as Diwali, Holi, Christmas, Eid, Ganesh Chaturthi and Durga Puja with our family, friends and neighbours.

Christmas

Eid

Children celebrating different festivals

FIND OUT
Think of other special days that you celebrate as a family.

CONCEPT MAP

My Family

types:

- Small family
  - has: father, mother and child/children
- Big family
  - has: father, mother, children, grandparents, aunts, uncles and cousins

Neighbourhood

(Area around our house)

Neighbours

(People who live near our house)

should:

- be friendly
- be helpful
- never fight
- celebrate festivals together

KEYWORDS

Family: a group of people living together

Neighbours: people who live near our house

Neighbourhood: places around our house

Festivals: special days that people celebrate with their family and friends

Exercise

Objective Type Questions

A. Choose the correct answer.

1. You should not ____________ with your neighbours.
   a. help b. fight c. visit d. talk
2. A small family has a father, mother and ____________.
   a. cousins b. uncles c. aunts d. children
3. ____________ is an indoor game.
   a. Football b. Cricket c. Tennis d. Carrom
4. A family having eight members is a ____________ family.
   a. small b. nuclear c. single-parent d. large
5. We can ____________ to have fun with our family in the weekends.
   a. play games b. study c. sleep d. visit the doctor

B. Fill in the blanks.

1. Mother, father and children make a ________________ (family/party).
2. Big families have ________________ (four/more than four) members.
3. Your father's parents are your ________________ (grandparents/uncles).
4. ________________ (Neighbours/Cousins) live near our house.
5. We should never ________________ (have fun/fight) with our neighbours.

C. Write T for True and F for False.

1. All families are small. ◯
2. Grandchildren can only be boys. ◯
3. Your uncle's children are your cousins. ◯
4. Family members should help each other. ◯

Subjective Type Questions

A. Choose the odd one out. Give reasons for the choice.

1. Ludo	Chess	Snakes and Ladder	Cricket
2. Diwali	Birthday	Eid	Christmas
3. Teacher	Brother	Sister	Cousin
4. Dog	Cat	Rabbit	Wolf

B. Answer the following questions.

1. How many members are there in your family?

____

____

2. Do you have a small or a big family?

____

3. Write two fun things that you do with your family on weekends.

____

4. Which is your favourite festival and why?

____

5. What are pets?

____

Application-based Questions

A. Riya lives with her father, mother and brother. Is her family small or big?

B. Hazel has two brothers and a sister. They live with their mother, father, grandmother and grandfather. How many members are there in Hazel's family?

Picture-based Question

Identify and name the types of families shown in the following pictures.

Skill Booster

A. 21CS: Creativity and Innovation | AI | BT: Affective, Psychomotor

Paste pictures of all your family members in your scrapbook. Below the picture of each member, write about your relationship with that member and why you love him or her. Decorate your scrapbook and show it to your friends and teacher.

B. 21CS: Critical Thinking, Life Skills | BT: Cognitive, Affective

Your father brings home a big chocolate bar. Your sister has gone out to play. What will you do? Tick (✔) the correct option.

☐ Eat the whole chocolate bar before she comes back.

☐ Wait for your sister to come back and then share the chocolate bar with her.

Worksheet 2

My SEE Journal

A. What games do you play with your friends?

B. Paste a picture of yourself with your best friend.

My SDG Journal

5 GENDER EQUALITY

A. Do you help your family members? Give one example.

B. Do you have friends in your neighbourhood? Write their names.

3 My Needs: Food We Eat

Prior Knowledge

- Names of some common food items
- Healthy food

Learning Objectives

- Need for food
- Sources of food
- Meals of the day
- Food for different age groups
- Healthy eating habits
- Eating manners

LET'S GET STARTED

Sasha is hungry. She is thinking of different food items but cannot decide what to eat. Help her decide which food she should eat.

NEED FOR FOOD

We eat food to live, grow, stay healthy and strong.

Food gives us the energy that we need to work and play.

SOURCES OF FOOD

We get our food from plants and animals.

We eat fruits and vegetables that we get from plants. People who eat food obtained from plants only are called **vegetarians**.

Vegetables

Fruits

Food obtained from plants

TALK TIME

- How do you feel when you are sick and do not eat properly for a day or two?
- Should you eat only the food that you like? (Yes/No) Why?
- What is your favourite food?

We get food such as meat, eggs and milk from animals. People who eat meat are called **non-vegetarians**.

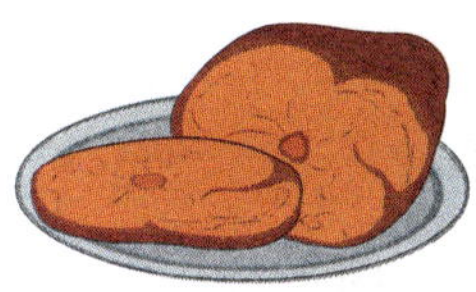

Meat

Eggs

Milk

Food items obtained from animals

RAW AND COOKED FOOD

Food can be eaten in **raw** (uncooked) and **cooked** forms. Some vegetables such as carrot, cucumber, mint and all fruits and nuts can be eaten raw. Some food items are cooked so that they become soft and tasty. Cereals, pulses, eggs, meat and rice are eaten in their cooked forms.

Raw food

Cooked food

Some of the food items can be eaten both raw and cooked. Onion, tomato, cabbage, papaya and banana are some of the food items that can be eaten both in raw and cooked forms.

QUICK REVISION

A. Look at the pictures below and write whether we get the following items from plants (P) or animals (A).

eggs ◯

bread ◯

meat ◯

tomato soup ◯

B. Sort the food items given below into three categories: eaten raw, eaten cooked and can be eaten both raw and cooked.

cucumber mango carrot radish apple egg fish beans
tomato pear meat brinjal peas potato grapes banana

FOOD FOR DIFFERENT AGE GROUPS

Sometimes, different food is given to different people. Very small babies are given milk as they have no teeth. When babies start eating food, they are given special soft food. This food helps babies grow. As we grow up and get teeth, we are given food that needs to be chewed.

A baby drinking milk

An old man having a special diet

When we fall ill, we need to eat a special **diet** as told by the doctor. This type of food helps us recover from the sickness and get healthy again. Sometimes, elderly people also need to eat a special diet regularly. This diet may be food that is soft and easy to chew and not spicy at all.

We must remember to eat healthy food at all times.

> **WORD TO KNOW**
> diet: a type of food that we regularly eat

MEALS OF THE DAY

We should take our meals regularly. Meal is the food that we eat at a certain time during the day. The three main meals are breakfast, lunch and dinner.

Breakfast in the morning

Lunch in the afternoon

Dinner at night

HEALTHY EATING HABITS

- We must always eat fresh and clean food. If we do not eat fresh food, we may fall sick.
- We must drink enough water.
- We must eat healthy food and avoid eating too much junk food such as crisps, pizzas, chocolates and ice creams. They can make us fat and unhealthy.

Healthy food

EATING MANNERS

- Take as much food as you can eat and do not waste food.
- Always eat with your mouth closed.
- Wait for everybody to be served before you start eating.
- Do not play with the **cutlery**.
- Do not make noise while eating.

A family having a meal together

WORD TO KNOW
cutlery: spoon, fork and knife

CONCEPT MAP

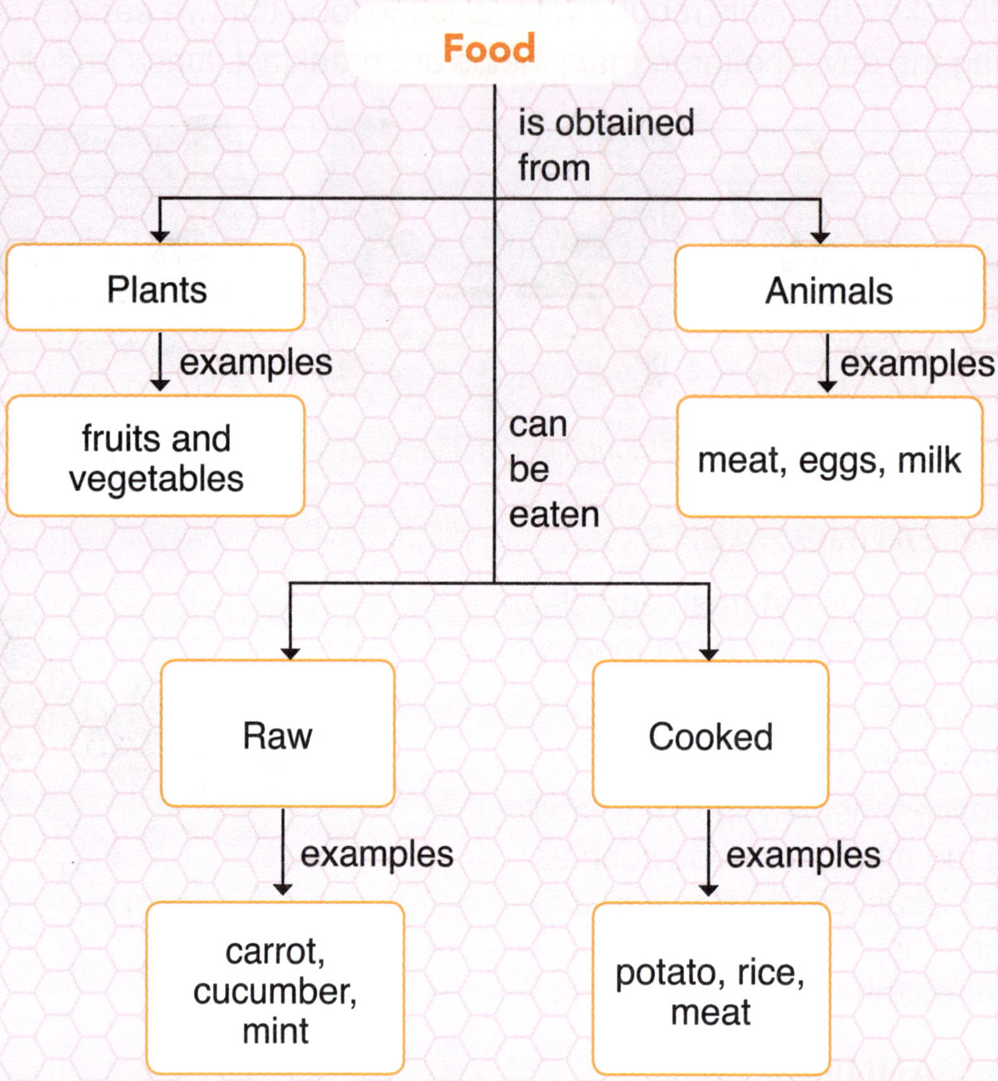

KEYWORDS

Vegetarians: people who eat food obtained from plants only

Non-vegetarians: people who eat food such as meat and eggs along with food obtained from plants

Raw food: food eaten without cooking such as carrot and cucumber

Meal: the food that we eat at a certain time during the day

Exercise

Objective Type Questions

A. Choose the correct answer.

1. Food makes us ____________.
   a. strong b. weak c. meek d. timid
2. We get ____________ from plants.
   a. fruits b. eggs c. milk d. meat
3. A person who eats only food obtained from plants is called a ____________.
   a. vegetarian b. non-vegetarian
   c. fruit seller d. baker
4. There are ____________ main meals.
   a. five b. three
   c. two d. four
5. We should eat with our mouth ____________.
   a. closed b. open c. half open d. half closed

B. Fill in the blanks.

1. We should always eat ____________ (fresh/stale) food.
2. We must drink plenty of ____________ (cold drinks/water).
3. Eating too much ____________ (junk food/fruits) is unhealthy.
4. We must always chew with our ____________ (eyes/mouth) closed.

Subjective Type Questions

A. Differentiate between the following.

1. Vegetarians and non-vegetarians
2. Raw and cooked food

B. Answer the following questions.

1. Why do we need to eat food?

   ____

   ____

2. Where do we get our food from?

   ____

3. Name the three main meals.

   ____

4. Why should we avoid eating too much junk food?

   ____

5. Write any two table manners.

   ____

   ____

Application-based Questions

A. Abhishek skips his breakfast every day because he is always in a hurry to reach school on time. Do you think he will stay healthy if he continues to skip his breakfast?

B. Raghu has a four-month-old sister. Raghu gets rice, chapati and vegetables for dinner, but his sister only gets milk. Why?

Picture-based Question

Colour the healthy food green and the junk food red.

Burger

Carrot

Cake

Doughnut

Skill Booster

A. 21CS: Life Skills | BT: Cognitive, Affective

You are having dinner at a friend's house. You don't like some of the dishes served. What would you do? Tick (✔) the correct option.

- ☐ Say you do not like it.
- ☐ Taste a little.
- ☐ Take the food but do not eat it.

B. 21CS: Life Skills | EL | BT: Psychomotor

I Am a Chef Today!

Things you will need: Two bread slices, some basil leaves, grated carrot, grated cucumber, grated cheese, two spoons mayonnaise, a pinch of salt and a pinch of black pepper

Let us start: Mix all the ingredients in a bowl. Take some mixture in a spoon and spread on one bread slice. Put the other bread slice over it. Your healthy sandwich is ready!

C. 21CS: Information Literacy | IF | BT: Affective

During different festivals, different special dishes are prepared in different parts of India. For example, *halwa* on Gurpurab, *sewaiyan* on Eid, cake on Christmas and *gujia* on Holi. Name the main festivals celebrated in your state and the special dishes prepared for them.

Worksheet 3

Naro's mother gives him healthy food.

Jimmy is a poor child.

My SEE Journal

A. Is it okay to waste food? How do your parents feel when you don't eat your food?

____

____

____

____

____

B. How do you feel when you see someone wasting food? Tick a smiley that shows how you feel.

 ◯

 ◯

My SDG Journal

2 ZERO HUNGER

A. What can you do to help children who do not have enough food to eat?

____

____

____

____

B. Draw your favourite dish and colour it.

4 My Needs: Water

Prior Knowledge

- Need for water to live
- Uses of water: drinking, bathing, cooking
- Need for water for plants

Learning Objectives

- Sources of water
- Uses of water
- Fun with water
- Saving water

LET'S GET STARTED

Look at the pictures shown below. Which of the following animals live in water? Put a tick (✔) or a cross (✘) in the boxes given below the pictures.

1. 

2. 

3. 

4. 

All plants, animals and human beings need water to live.

SOURCES OF WATER

Sources of water

Rain is the main source of all the water on the Earth.

Other sources of water are rivers, ponds, lakes and seas. These sources are filled up by rainwater.

Some rainwater also **seeps** into the ground. We dig wells or use hand pumps to take this water out from under the ground. We get water in our houses through taps. Some houses have wells.

At home, we store water in bottles, pots and buckets. Large amounts of water are stored in water tanks and dams.

We should always drink clean water. If we do not drink clean water, we fall sick.

> **WORD TO KNOW**
> seep: to pass or flow through something

DO YOU KNOW?

Clean water has
- No colour
- No smell
- No taste
- No shape

WATER MAGIC

Take a bottle of water. Now, pour some water into a glass. Wow! The shape of water changes into the shape of the glass. This shows that water takes the shape of the vessel it is poured into.

USES OF WATER

- We use water for cooking, drinking, bathing and washing clothes.
- Animals need water for drinking and bathing.
- Plants also need water to grow and live.
- A fireman uses water to put out fire.

Cooking

Watering plants

Fireman putting out fire

QUICK REVISION

Fill in the blanks.

1. All plants, animals and human beings need __________ to live.
2. At home, we store water in ________, _________ and _________.
3. Animals need water for __________ and __________.
4. A fireman uses water to put out __________.

FUN WITH WATER

We use water for various fun activities such as boating, sailing paper boats, swimming, water slides and diving under water to see the animals living there.

Water games

Sailing paper boat

Enjoying on the water slide

Diving under water

Some water activities

SAVING WATER

Water is useful to us in many ways. We must not waste water. Here are a few ways to save water.

We should close the tap properly after use.

We should use a bucket and a mug to take a bath.

We should not keep the tap running while brushing our teeth.

REUSE OF WATER

- We can use the water left in the bucket after a bath to water plants.
- The rainwater can be used to clean and wash cars and to water plants.

CONCEPT MAP

Water

sources ↓

rain, rivers, lakes, ponds

uses ↓

- We need water for cooking, drinking, bathing and washing.
- Animals need water for drinking and bathing.
- Plants need water to grow and to live.
- Fireman uses water to put out fire.

ways to save water ↓

- Close the tap after use.
- Use a bucket and mug to bathe.
- Do not keep the tap running while brushing teeth.

KEYWORDS

Groundwater: water that is found under the ground

Dams: large walls built on rivers to store water

Exercise

Objective Type Questions

A. Choose the correct answer.

1. ____________ is the main source of water on the Earth.
   a. Ocean b. River c. Rain d. Dam
2. To save water, we should not ____________.
   a. close the tap b. bathe
   c. use rainwater to water plants d. waste water
3. Water is not used for ____________.
   a. cooking b. washing c. bathing d. para-gliding
4. Water has ____________.
   a. colour b. mass c. taste d. shape
5. We need water to ____________.
   a. sew b. bathe c. dry clothes d. kill insects

B. Write T for True and F for False.

1. All plants need water to live. ◯
2. Water has no shape. ◯
3. We get water from animals. ◯
4. We should always drink clean water. ◯
5. We must save water. ◯

C. Match the following.

1. Underground water	a. Fireman
2. Storage of water	b. Plants
3. Need water to grow	c. Bucket
4. Puts out fire with water	d. Well

Subjective Type Questions

A. Choose the odd one out. Give reasons for the choice.

1. Boating	Swimming	Diving	Drinking
2. Bucket	Tank	Tap	Bottle
3. Digging	Cooking	Washing	Bathing
4. River	Lake	Pond	Fridge
5. Plants	Stones	Animals	Humans

B. Answer the following questions.

1. Name any two sources of water.

2. Write two ways of saving water.

3. Write two uses of water.

4. Write any two fun activities related to water.

5. How do we take out water from under the ground?

Application-based Questions

A. Renu went on a picnic and drank water from the pond. She got very sick after that. What do you think could be the reason?

B. Gautham collects the water left in the glasses of each family member after dinner. He uses it to water the plants in his garden. Is it a good habit or a bad habit? Why? What do you do with the water left in your school water bottle?

Picture-based Questions

A. Which of the following needs water?

Plant

Football

Sailboat

B. Write the names of the following water games with the help of the word box.

swimming	fishing	boating	diving under water

Skill Booster

A. **21CS:** Critical Thinking | **AI** | **BT:** Cognitive, Psychomotor

Colour the drops of water and write one use of water in each drop.

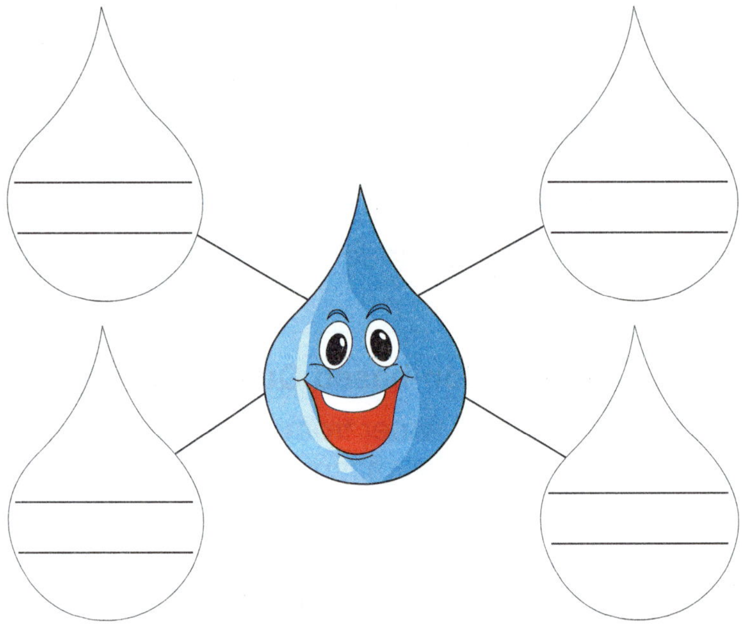

B. **21CS:** Critical Thinking | **AI** | **BT:** Affective, Psychomotor

Colour the picture of the aquarium given below.

_______________ and _______________ also live in water.

Worksheet 4

Jamie is enjoying his shower for more than an hour

Abhi is bathing using a bucket and a mug.

My SEE Journal

A. What is the difference between the two pictures?

____

____

____

____

____

____

B. Why should we save water?

____

____

____

____

____

____

My SDG Journal

6 CLEAN WATER AND SANITATION

A. Do you keep the tap open while brushing teeth? Colour the circle Red if Yes and Green if No.

B. Write one way by which you save water at home.

____

____

____

____

____

5 My Needs: Shelter

Prior Knowledge

- Home: A place where we live
- Small and big houses

Learning Objectives

- Need for a house
- Types of houses
- Keeping our homes clean
- Decorating our homes

LET'S GET STARTED

Match the following animals with their homes.

1 

a 

2 

b 

3 

c 

NEED FOR A HOUSE

A house is a place where we live with our family. A house gives us shelter and protects us from heat, cold, rain, thieves and animals.

A house protects us from heat and rain.

A POEM!

This is my house
And this is me,
God bless the house
And God bless me!
I live here with my family
It is where I am most happy,
I read, rest, sing and play
And have fun the whole day!

A house may have one room or many rooms. Each room has its own use. Look at the picture given below to learn about the different rooms in a house and their uses.

Different rooms in a house

QUICK REVISION

Match the following.

1. The room where we sleep and rest	a. Study room
2. The room where we study	b. Kitchen
3. The room where we cook food	c. Bedroom

TYPES OF HOUSES

People live in different types of houses.

A bungalow

A hut

An apartment

Different types of houses

DO YOU KNOW?

An architect is a person who plans and looks after a house while it gets built.

KEEPING OUR HOMES CLEAN

It is important to keep our house neat and clean. Here are some ways to do this.

- Throwing litter in the dustbin
- Putting away our toys back in place after playing
- Keeping our book shelf and study table neat
- Keeping our shoes on the shoe rack
- Putting the dirty clothes in the correct place for washing

A boy throwing litter in the dustbin

A boy putting toys back in place

DECORATING OUR HOMES

We decorate our homes to make them look beautiful.

During festivals, we decorate our homes with lights, diyas, flowers and by making *rangolis*.

TALK TIME

What else can you do to keep your house clean?

Children decorating their house with lights

CONCEPT MAP

House

different rooms
- Drawing room
- Bedroom
- Study room
- Kitchen
- Dining room
- Bathroom

protects us from
- Heat
- Cold
- Rain
- Thieves
- Animals

types
- A bungalow
- A hut
- An apartment

Different rooms in a house

KEYWORDS

House: the place where we live with our family

Shelter: a place where we can live safely

Exercise

Objective Type Questions

A. Choose the correct answer.

1. A house with many storeys is called __________.
   a. a tent b. an apartment
   c. a hut d. a caravan
2. An architect is a person who __________ the house.
   a. paints b. builds c. plans d. guards
3. We have meals together in a __________.
   a. kitchen b. drawing room
   c. dining room d. bedroom
4. __________ helps us keep our house clean.
   a. Littering b. Dancing
   c. Keeping shoes on the shoe rack d. Fighting with pillows
5. When guests come, we make them sit in the __________ room.
   a. drawing b. bed c. study d. dining

B. Fill in the blanks.

1. I sleep in my ______________ (bedroom/drawing room).
2. I bathe in the ______________ (study room/bathroom).
3. Mummy cooks food in the ______________ (drawing room/kitchen).
4. We spend time with friends in the ______________ (bedroom/drawing room).
5. We decorate our homes to make them look ____________ (untidy/beautiful).

Subjective Type Questions

A. Differentiate between the following.

1. Bedroom and drawing room
2. Kitchen and dining room
3. Study room and bathroom

B. Answer the following questions.

1. Write two ways to keep your house clean.

____

____

2. Why do we need a house?

____

____

3. Name any two rooms in a house and their use.

____

____

4. Why do we decorate our homes?

____

____

Application-based Question

My Home and My Senses

1. Two things that I see in my home
2. Two things that I smell in my home
3. Two things in my home that I can touch
4. Two things in my home that I hear

Picture-based Question

Draw a picture of your home and decorate it.

Skill Booster

A. **21CS:** Life Skills | **EL** | **BT:** Cognitive, Affective

Tick (✔) the things you do when you return home from school.

- ☐ Put your bag in the room.
- ☐ Put your clothes in the basin for wash.
- ☐ Put your socks in the wash basin.
- ☐ Put your shoes on the shoe rack.
- ☐ Wash your handkerchief.

B. **21CS:** Critical Thinking | **BT:** Cognitive, Psychomotor

Put the following in the right room of the house.

Bed

Television

Bedroom	Drawing room	Kitchen	Bathroom

Chest of drawers

Wash basin

Sofa

Mixer

Bucket

Toaster

Worksheet 5

Jahan, Jahnavi and their dad are preparing lunch as their mom is finishing some urgent office work.

My SEE Journal

A. 'Family members should help, care and support each other.' Do you agree or disagree with this statement? Why or why not?

B. Make a sandwich for your mother. Write two items you will use to make the sandwich.

My SDG Journal

17 PARTNERSHIPS FOR THE GOALS

A. Do you help your parents? How?

B. After coming back from school, what do you do with your school uniform and shoes?

6 My Needs: Clothing

Prior Knowledge

- Names of some common clothing: shirts, trousers, jackets, frocks and skirts
- School uniform

Learning Objectives

- Need for clothes
- Clothes for different seasons
- Special clothes
- Care of clothes

LET'S GET STARTED

Write the names of the clothing shown below. Take help from the word box.

hat	sweater	frock	gloves

1. 

   ____

2. 

   ____

3. 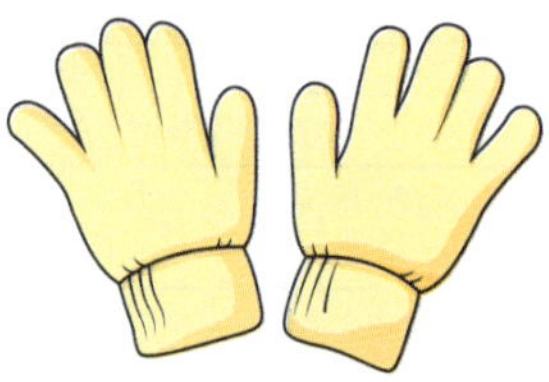

   ____

4. 

   ____

Clothes are the things that people wear. Shirts, trousers, skirts, coats, frocks and saris are some examples of clothes.

NEED FOR CLOTHES

We wear clothes to cover our body. They protect us from heat, cold, wind, rain and insect bites. Clothes make us look smart too!

Make your motto: **Look Good, Feel Good!**

> How does a raincoat save our clothes from getting wet in the rain?
>
> 
>
> **FIND OUT**

CLOTHES FOR DIFFERENT SEASONS

We wear different clothes for different seasons.

In summer, when it is very hot, we wear light **cotton clothes**.

In monsoons, when it rains, we wear a **raincoat**. A raincoat is waterproof. It does not soak in water like our other clothes.

In winter, when it is cold, we wear **woollen clothes**.

Summer

Monsoon

Winter

Different clothes for different seasons

SPECIAL CLOTHES

Just as we wear a uniform to school, some people wear special clothes to work.

> **WORD TO KNOW**
>
> fireproof: something that does not catch fire

We wear a ***uniform*** *to school.*

A doctor wears a ***white coat****.*

A fireman wears a ***fireproof uniform****.*

A soldier wears a ***uniform****.*

QUICK REVISION

What would you wear on a hot day? Circle the correct pictures.

CLOTHES WORN AT HOME

We wear comfortable clothes at home. We wear loose fitting clothes when we go to sleep at night. It is called a **night dress**.

Children wearing comfortable clothes

A family wearing comfortable clothes

TALK TIME

What do you like to wear at home?

Clothes Worn on Special Days

We dress properly for different occasions such as outings, festivals and birthdays.

Clothes for an outing at the beach

Clothes for Diwali

Clothes for a birthday party

CARE OF CLOTHES

We must wear clean clothes at all times. To keep our clothes clean, we should do the following.

- Put our clothes in the wash every day
- Iron and fold our clothes properly

Taking care of clothes

CONCEPT MAP

Clothes

In summer, we wear light cotton clothes.

In monsoon, when it rains, we wear a raincoat.

In winter, we wear woollen clothes.

KEYWORDS

Clothes: things that people wear to protect themselves from heat, cold and rain

Cotton clothes: light clothes that we wear in summer

Woollen clothes: clothes that we wear in winter

Raincoat: waterproof coat that we wear on a rainy day to protect ourselves from getting wet by rain

Uniform: special clothes that some people wear to work

Exercise

Objective Type Questions

A. Choose the correct answer.

1. We wear __________ clothes in summer season.
   a. silk b. cotton c. woollen d. waterproof
2. A __________ wears a uniform.
   a. fireman b. tailor c. fisherman d. gardener
3. A woollen dress keeps us __________.
   a. cool b. warm c. waterproof d. wet
4. Clothes should be __________.
   a. too tight b. too loose
   c. comfortable d. uncomfortable
5. We wear a swimsuit when we go to __________.
   a. the hills b. a forest
   c. a beach d. the mountains

B. Fill in the blanks.

1. When it is cold, we wear __________ (cotton/woollen) clothes.
2. We wear clothes to __________ (cover/clean) our body.
3. We wear a __________ (fancy dress/uniform) to school every day.

C. Write T for True and F for False.

1. We wear a raincoat when it is cold. ◯
2. We wear comfortable clothes at home. ◯
3. We wear fancy clothes to school. ◯
4. We dress properly for different occasions. ◯

Subjective Type Questions

A. Choose the odd one out. Give reasons for the choice.

1. Sweater	Swimsuit	Coat	Jacket
2. Paper	Cotton	Silk	Wool
3. Raincoat	Umbrella	Gumboots	Sweater
4. Shirt	School bag	Shorts	Belt
5. Button	Pocket	Shoes	Collar

B. Answer the following questions.

1. Why do we wear clothes?

____

2. What type of clothes do we wear in summer?

____

3. Write two ways in which you can take care of your clothes.

____

Application-based Question

Rishi is going for an outing from school. The sky is covered with dark clouds. What do you think he should remember to carry?

Picture-based Question

Look at the picture and answer the following questions.

1. What is the child wearing?
2. In which season do we wear these type of clothes?
3. Do you like this season? Why or why not?

Skill Booster

A. 21CS: Life Skills | BT: Cognitive

What do you think Soham should do once he returns from an exciting football match? Tick (✔) the correct answer.

- [ ] Lie in bed and rest without changing clothes.
- [ ] Have a bath and wear fresh clothes.

B. 21CS: Life Skills | BT: Affective, Psychomotor

Nitin was cleaning his cupboard. He took out all those clothes that no longer fitted him. What do you think can be done with the clothes. Tick (✔) the correct options.

- [ ] He can use the old ones for dusting.
- [ ] He can just throw away all the old clothes.
- [ ] He can donate the old clothes to people who need them.

Worksheet 6

My SEE Journal

A. What type of a girl is Amy? Write in one word.

____

B. What type of a girl or a boy are you?

____

____

____

C. Draw your favourite dress and colour it.

My SDG Journal

12 RESPONSIBLE CONSUMPTION AND PRODUCTION

A. What will you do with your old clothes that you no longer wear?

____

____

____

____

____

B. Apart from giving away clothes, what other things can you do to help others?

____

____

____

____

____

____

7

My Needs: Air

Prior Knowledge

- Air helps in breathing
- Names of a few things that fly in the air such as kites, aeroplanes and helicopters

Learning Objectives

- Air
- Uses of air
- Plants help clean the air
- Keeping the air clean

LET'S GET STARTED

Look at the picture and answer the questions given below it.

1. Circle the two things that move in the air.
2. Can these things move in a closed room? Yes/No

You are right! Pinwheel and kite move in the air and these cannot move in a closed room. Do you know why? This is because air helps in moving the kite and pinwheel. In a closed room, the air is there but it is not moving. Only moving air can make things move.

Let us learn more about air in this chapter.

AIR

Strong wind

Air is all around us but we cannot see it. This is because air has no colour.

We can feel the air when it moves.

Moving air is called **wind**. Strong winds can blow away things and may also hurt human beings.

USES OF AIR

Air helps us in many ways.

- Plants, animals and human beings need air to breathe.
- Air is also filled in footballs, tyres of cars and bicycles, airbeds and balloons to give them shape.
- Air helps things fly.
- Air helps windmills and sailboats move.
- Air helps in drying wet clothes.
- Air helps in burning things. For example, a candle will not burn if there is no air.

Filling air in the tyre of a car

Windmill

Drying clothes

QUICK REVISION

Fill in the blanks.

1. Moving air is called _______________.
2. Living beings need air to _______________.
3. Air helps in _______________ wet clothes.

PLANTS HELP CLEAN THE AIR

Plants absorb the harmful things present in the air. They also give out oxygen that we need to breathe. Hence, they help clean the air. The more trees we plant, the cleaner the air is around us.

KEEPING THE AIR CLEAN

Sometimes, air becomes dirty because of dust and smoke from factories, vehicles, burning of dry leaves and bursting of firecrackers. Breathing in dirty air makes us ill.

People, plants and animals need clean air to breathe and stay healthy. To keep the air clean, we should take the following steps.

- Plant more trees
- Walk short distances or ride a bicycle instead of going by a car
- Do not burn dry leaves or garbage

TALK TIME

In this picture, you can see a man wearing a mask. Why do you think he is wearing the mask?

Children planting a tree

Children riding bicycles

GREENATHON

Collect dry leaves from the garden or park. Put them in a wooden box containing soil. Cover the leaves with more soil and sprinkle water on it. Cover the box with a lid. After every 3-4 days, mix the contents and sprinkle water. Wait for 3–4 months. Your compost is ready! Spread it in the soil of your garden or planters. It will make your plants healthy and grow fast.

CONCEPT MAP

Air

Air is all around us. We cannot see it, but we can feel it.

Uses of Air

- Living things need air to breathe.
- Air helps things fly.
- Air is used to fill tyres, footballs and balloons.
- Air helps in burning.
- Air helps dry wet clothes.
- Air moves windmills and sailboats.

- Plants help keep the air clean.

KEYWORDS

Wind: the moving air that we can feel

Oxygen: the component of the air that we take in through our nose when we breathe

Exercise

Objective Type Questions

A. Choose the correct answer.

1. A ____________ does not need air to move.
   a. sailboat b. kite c. scooter d. windmill
2. Moving air is called ____________.
   a. oxygen b. storm c. wind d. gale
3. ____________ needs air.
   a. Burning b. Watching cartoons
   c. Freezing d. Diving
4. Dirty air is ____________ for us.
   a. harmful b. good c. colourful d. useful
5. Plants give out ____________.
   a. nitrogen b. oxygen c. carbon dioxide d. hydrogen

B. Write T for True and F for False.

1. We can see the air around us. ◯
2. Plants do not need air. ◯
3. Dirty air can be bad for our health. ◯
4. Air is white in colour. ◯

Subjective Type Questions

A. Give reasons for the following.

1. We cannot see the air.
2. We should breathe in clean air.
3. We should plant more trees.

B. Answer the following questions.

1. What is wind?

   ____

2. Write two ways in which air helps us.

   ____

3. What makes air dirty?

   ____

Application-based Question

Raju's football has become soft and does not bounce anymore. What does he need to do to make it bounce again?

Picture-based Question

Circle the items that need air.

1. 

Football

2. 

Sheep

3. 

Pencil

Skill Booster

A. **21CS:** Creativity and Innovation | **AI** | **BT:** Psychomotor

Colour the kite given below.

B. **21CS:** Critical Thinking, Life Skills | **BT:** Cognitive, Affective

We can help in keeping the air clean by taking simple steps.

- We should walk or use a cycle instead of a car as much as possible.
- We should not burn wood.
- We should plant more trees.

Write two more steps to keep the air clean.

Worksheet 7

My SEE Journal

A. What is the family talking about?

B. Do you also discuss things like this with your family? Give one example.

My SDG Journal

A. Write two reasons of air pollution.

B. Write one way by which you can prevent air pollution.

8 Keeping Oneself Clean, Safe and Healthy

Prior Knowledge

- Cleanliness
- Keeping healthy

Learning Objectives

- Personal hygiene
- Toilet manners
- Exercise and rest
- Being safe
- Good or bad touch

LET'S GET STARTED

Look at the pictures given below and circle the things you need to keep yourself clean.

1. 
Soap

2. 
Book

3. 
Pencil

4. 
Toothbrush

Look at the things shown below and circle the things that you should never play with.

1. 
Matchbox

2. 
Pinwheel

3. 
Scissors

4. 
Ball

Very good! You answered both the questions correctly. In this chapter, we will learn about the importance of cleanliness and the safety rules that we should follow at different places to keep ourselves safe from getting hurt.

PERSONAL HYGIENE

To stay healthy, we must keep ourselves clean and fit.

We brush our teeth.

We go to the toilet.

We take a bath.

We wear clean clothes.

We comb our hair.

We wash our hands before and after meals.

We clip our nails.

Always use a handkerchief while coughing and sneezing. It stops the germs from spreading.

We do not have to wear **expensive** clothes to look good. We only have to wear clean clothes.

WORD TO KNOW

expensive: something that costs a lot of money

TOILET MANNERS

A toilet should always be kept clean. It stops the germs from spreading. Some toilet manners are given below.

- Always keep the toilet dry.
- Flush after using the toilet.
- Make sure the toilet seat is clean after use.
- Wash your hands after using the toilet.
- Stand close to the basin while washing your hands or mouth.
- Do not waste water.

Toilet seat should be clean after use.

Cleanliness in the House and Surroundings

Dirty surroundings make us ill. It is important to keep our surroundings clean. We spend most of our time either at home or in school. That is why, we should keep our homes and school clean. The garbage should be thrown in the garbage bins. We should also plant more trees.

Boy throwing waste in garbage bin

EXERCISE AND REST

We know that we should eat healthy food and also keep our body clean to stay healthy. But do you know that it is important to exercise and rest too? Our body grows properly if we exercise and take proper rest.

TALK TIME
Which is your favourite exercise?

Some forms of exercises for children are given here.

Doing yoga

Jogging

Playing

Stretching

Swimming

Cycling

Our body also needs rest. If we do not get enough rest, we will feel tired. We must go to bed early and wake up early. We need at least eight hours of sleep every night.

BEING SAFE

In our daily life, we come across many things that can hurt us. So, we should always be careful of such things and stay safe from getting hurt or injured. Protecting ourselves from danger or things that might hurt us is called **safety**.

Safety Rules

To keep ourselves safe, we should follow some rules. These rules are called **safety rules**. We should follow safety rules at all times and everywhere. Let us learn about the safety rules that we should follow at different places.

Safety at Home

- We should not play with sharp things. They may hurt us.
- We should not play with electric wires or electrical objects. They may give us a shock.
- We should keep our toys in place after playing with them. Otherwise, someone might step on them and fall.
- We should not play with matchsticks. They might spark off a fire.

A girl playing with sharp objects

A boy playing with an electrical socket

Toys not kept in place

Safety on the Road

It is very important to be careful on the road. To protect ourselves from accidents on the road, we must follow the safety rules given below.

- Never run or play on the road.
- Always walk on the footpath meant for walkers. A footpath is a narrow path on the side of the road.
- Before crossing a road, look to the right, then to the left and then to the right again. Cross only when the road is clear. Always hold your parents' or an elder's hand while crossing the road.
- Always cross the road at a **zebra crossing**. These are black and white stripes at some places on the road.
- Obey the traffic light signals. The red light tells you to stop, the yellow light tells you to wait and the green light tells you to go.

Girl walking on the footpath

People crossing the road at a zebra crossing

TALK TIME

Chiya saw a man talking on the mobile phone while crossing the road. Was the man doing the right thing? Why or why not?

QUICK REVISION

Write T for True and F for False.

1. We must follow safety rules at all times. ◯
2. We can play with matchsticks. ◯
3. We can play in the middle of the road. ◯
4. We should cross the road only at a zebra crossing. ◯

Safety in the Bus

- Sit quietly on your seat. Do not move around when the bus is running.
- Do not stand in a moving bus.
- Do not shout in a moving bus; it disturbs the driver.
- Keep the bus clean.
- Do not get into or get down from a moving bus.
- Never put your arm or head out of the bus window.
- Stand in a queue while waiting to get into the bus.

Children standing in a queue to get into the bus

Safety at School

- Do not play with sharp things such as a pointed pencil, scissors, ruler or sharpener.
- Do not run in the classroom; you might hurt yourself.
- Always walk in a line and do not push each other.
- Do not run in the **corridors**.

Students running in the classroom

WORD TO KNOW
corridor: a narrow passage

Safety in the Playground

- Do not fight with your friends.
- Do not stand in front of the swing when your friend is playing on the swing.
- Wait for your turn to play on a swing or a seesaw.

Wait for your turn for playing on a seesaw.

A POEM!

Always follow safety rules
To keep yourself safe
Watch your step, while walking
Tie up your shoe lace!
In the house or in the bus
Park or road or school,
We must always keep in mind
Being safe is very cool!

GOOD OR BAD TOUCH

How do you feel when your parents or friends hug you or touch your cheeks with love? Yes, you like it. A hug from your parents or your grandparents that makes you feel safe and happy is a **good touch**.

A good touch

A **bad touch** is when someone touches you and you do not feel comfortable or when the touch hurts you.

You should do the following things when someone touches you in a bad way.

- **Shout 'No' loudly**. Tell the person that you do not like to be touched.
- **Go away** from that person whose touch you do not like.
- **Tell** your parents or teachers whenever you feel a bad touch.
- Do not keep it as a **secret**.

CONCEPT MAP

Ways to Keep Clean and Healthy

- Bathing everyday
- Brushing teeth
- Clipping nails
- Combing hair
- Wearing clean clothes
- Washing hands before and after meals
- Keeping the toilet clean
- Keeping our surroundings clean
- Regular exercise and rest
- Eating healthy food

Safety Rules

On the Road

- Walk on the footpath.
- Do not play on the road.
- Cross the road at a zebra crossing.

At Home

- Do not play with sharp things, electric wires or objects.
- Keep toys in place after playing.
- Do not play with matchsticks.

In the Bus

- Sit quietly on your seat.
- Do not stand or shout in a moving bus.
- Do not get in or get down from a moving bus.
- Never put your arms or hands out of the bus window.

At School

- Do not play with sharp things.
- Do not run in the classroom or the corridors.
- Always walk in a line.

In the Playground

- Do not fight with one another.
- Do not stand in front of a swing.
- Wait for your turn to play.

KEYWORDS

Germs: tiny creatures that cause sickness

Surroundings: everything around us

Garbage: trash or unwanted things

Footpath: a narrow path on the side of the road for walking

Zebra crossing: black and white stripes at some places on the road

Good touch: a touch from our parents, teachers and friends that makes us feel good

Bad touch: a touch from someone that makes us feel bad or the touch that hurts us

Exercise

Objective Type Questions

A. Choose the correct answer.

1. We need ____________ hours of sleep everyday.
   a. five b. six c. eight d. twelve
2. We should ____________ flush the toilet after using it.
   a. never b. always c. sometimes d. None of these
3. We should follow safety rules ____________.
   a. only at home b. only at school
   c. everywhere d. nowhere
4. While travelling in a moving bus, we must ____________.
   a. scream b. sit quietly
   c. stand d. put our hands out
5. _______ are tiny creatures that cause sickness.
   a. Garbage b. Trash c. Germs d. Disease

B. Fill in the blanks.

1. Stand ________________ (away/close) to the basin while washing your hands or mouth.
2. Our body needs ________________ (rest/no rest) and ________________ (no sleep/sleep) to stay healthy.
3. If we follow safety rules, we can avoid ______________ (getting hurt/falling sick).
4. Always cross the road at the ________________ (footpath/zebra crossing).
5. When someone touches you in a way that makes you feel uncomfortable, it is a ________________ (good/bad) touch.

C. Write T for True and F for False.

1. We do not need to take a bath daily. ◯
2. Taking rest is important for us. ◯
3. We should always walk on the footpath. ◯
4. We should only cross when the road is clear. ◯
5. We should stand in a moving bus and make noise. ◯

Subjective Type Questions

A. Define the following.

1. Safety
2. Safety rules
3. Good touch

B. Answer the following questions.

1. Write two things we do to keep ourselves clean.

____

____

2. Write two toilet manners.

____

____

3. What are the three things we need to stay healthy?

____

4. Why should we follow safety rules?

____

5. Why should we pick up toys after playing with them?

____

6. Write two safety rules we should follow while travelling in a bus.

____

____

Application-based Questions

A. What do you think will happen if you only watch TV and stop doing exercise? Find out and write the term used to describe people who watch TV for a long duration without any other physical activity.

B. Raja's football rolled on to the road and he ran to fetch it. His mother got angry. Why?

Picture-based Question

Look at the pictures given below and cross (✗) the ones that show actions that are not safe.

◯ 

Sahil is playing with matches.

◯ 

Shikha and Amit are walking on the footpath.

◯ 

Daljeet and Hiyang are running on the road.

Skill Booster

A. 21CS: Life Skills | BT: Cognitive, Affective

Checklist: Are You Clean?

Tick (✔) either yes or no.

1. Do you have a bath every day? (Yes/No)
2. Do you polish your shoes every morning before going to school? (Yes/No)
3. Do you wash your hands before meals? (Yes/No)
4. Do you rinse your mouth after every meal? (Yes/No)
5. Do you wear a clean uniform to school? (Yes/No)
6. Do you shampoo your hair once a week? (Yes/No)
7. Do you wash your hands after using the toilet? (Yes/No)
8. Do you change your toothbrush every few months? (Yes/No)

If your answer to all the eight questions is yes, then you are super clean.

If your answer to any of the six questions is yes, then you are clean.

If your answer to less than five questions is yes, you need to take better care of your body.

B. 21CS: Critical Thinking, Life Skills | BT: Cognitive

Where do you see these traffic signs? What does each sign mean?

C. 21CS: Creativity and Innovation | AI | BT: Psychomotor

Project

Make a toothbrush and toothpaste holder.

You will need: A small tin, printed or coloured cloth and glue

Let us start: With the help of an elder, cut the cloth to wrap around the tin. Paste the cloth around the tin using glue. Let it dry. Once it dries, put your toothbrush and toothpaste in it. Your toothbrush and toothpaste holder is ready!

Worksheet 8

My SEE Journal

A. Do you think the girl is wise? How do you know this?

____

____

____

____

____

B. Make a 'Help' or 'I Feel Unsafe' stamp.

My SDG Journal

16 PEACE, JUSTICE AND STRONG INSTITUTIONS

A. If a stranger gives you candies when your parents are not around, would you take the candies or not? Why or why not?

____

____

____

____

B. Suppose your parents are late to pick you up from school and an unknown person tells you that he would drop you home? Will you go with him? Why or why not?

____

____

____

____

9 Places in the Neighbourhood

Prior Knowledge

- Names of some people living in the neighbourhood
- Names of some common places such as shops, parks, hospitals, schools and banks

Learning Objectives

- Our neighbourhood
- People who help us
- People who keep our parks, roads and cities clean

LET'S GET STARTED

Bino is standing in her balcony and looking outside from there. Can you name a few places that Bino can see from her balcony?

____

____

____

OUR NEIGHBOURHOOD

Places that are found around our house form our **neighbourhood**.

People who live near our house are called **neighbours**.

When a family moves to a new house, they make sure that everything is close to the house. Here are some of the places that a good neighbourhood should have.

A **bank** *to keep our money safe*

A **supermarket/market** *to buy day-to-day things from*

A **school** *to study in*

A **hospital** *to go to when we are unwell*

A **police station** *to go to report a theft*

A **fire station** *to call for help if there is a fire*

A **post office** *to send letters and parcels from*

A **park** *to play and exercise*

TALK TIME

Which places do you have in your neighbourhood?

PEOPLE WHO HELP US

There are many people who help us every day. They make our lives easier and happy. Here are a few people who help us.

A **teacher** *teaches us.*

A **baker** *bakes cakes and pastries for us.*

A **farmer** *grows food for us.*

A **policeman** *keeps us safe.*

A **doctor** *treats us when we fall sick.*

FIND OUT

What do we call the person who treats our pet dog when it falls sick?

A **carpenter** *makes furniture for us.*

A **postman** *delivers our letters and parcels.*

A **barber** *cuts our hair.*

A **watchman** *guards our houses.*

A **fireman** *puts out fire.*

A **shopkeeper** *sells things we need.*

PEOPLE WHO KEEP OUR PARKS, ROADS AND CITY CLEAN

A **street cleaner** *cleans our streets and roads.*

A **garbage collector** *collects garbage from houses and streets.*

DO YOU KNOW?

Many people work hard to keep parks and other places clean so that we can have fun and enjoy ourselves outdoors. We must respect and thank everyone who makes our lives comfortable.

A **street light electrician** *repairs street lights on the roads.*

A **road worker** *builds and repairs roads.*

A **gardener** *keeps the garden clean and green.*

Remember, you can also help in keeping your neighbourhood clean by throwing the waste in dustbins.

We can keep our parks and gardens clean by not littering and making them dirty.

OTHERS WHO HELP US

There are many other people who help us in our daily lives.

We go to the **dentist** when we have a toothache.

A **bus driver** drives us to and from school.

A **chef** cooks for us in a restaurant.

A **tailor** stitches clothes for us.

QUICK REVISION

Who am I?

1. I deliver your letters. ______________
2. I guard your house. ______________
3. I grow food for you. ______________
4. I teach you in class. ______________

CONCEPT MAP

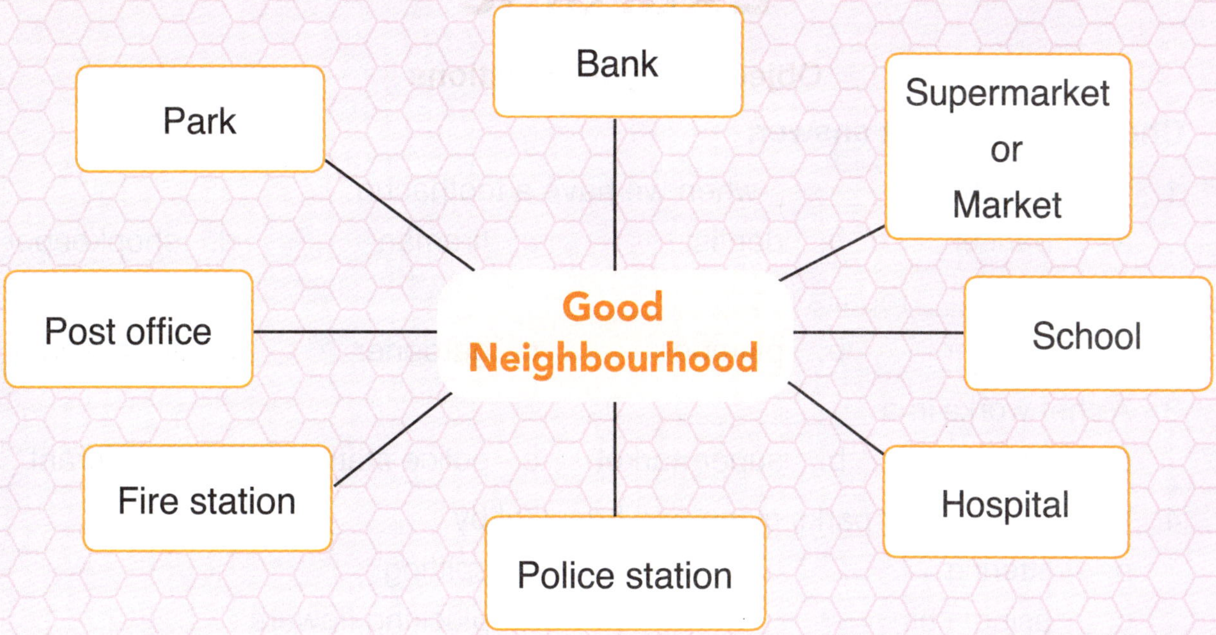

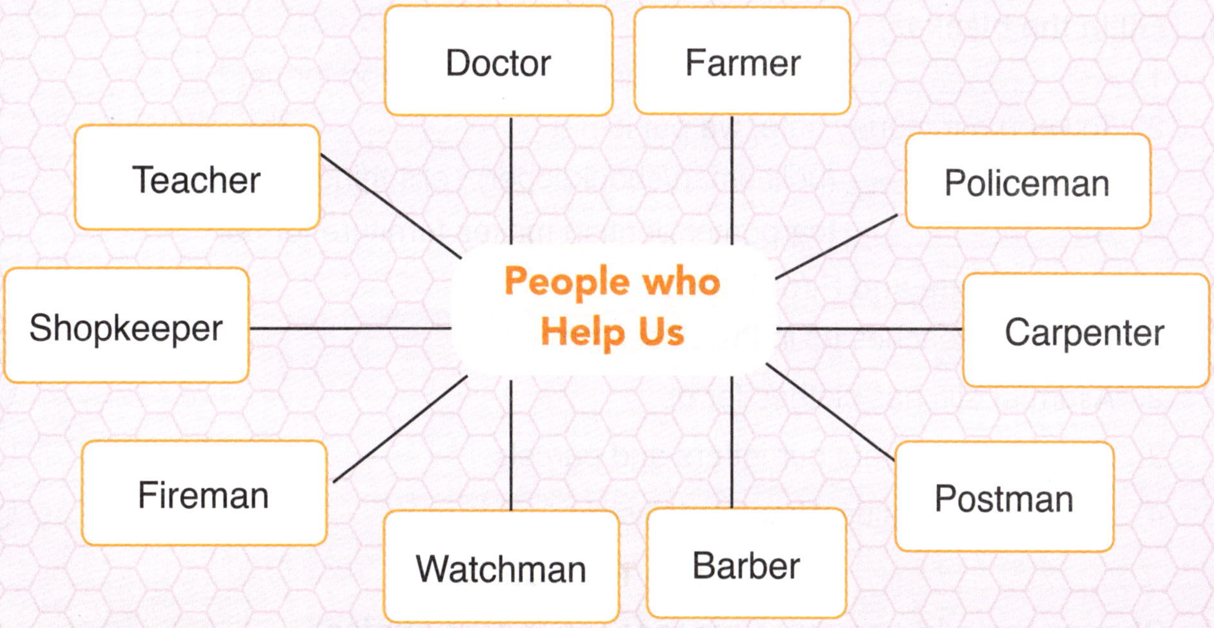

KEYWORDS

Neighbours: people who live near our house

Neighbourhood: all the places found around our house

Good neighbourhood: a neighbourhood that has all the places that we need

Exercise

Objective Type Questions

A. Choose the correct answer.

1. We go to the __________ when we have a toothache.
   a. banker b. dentist c. fireman d. shopkeeper
2. A ___________ repairs roads.
   a. cleaner b. plumber c. gardener d. road worker
3. A chef works in a ___________.
   a. bank b. supermarket c. police station d. restaurant
4. We can keep our parks clean and beautiful by ___________.
   a. littering b. spitting
   c. using a bin d. plucking flowers
5. We should respect a ___________.
   a. teacher b. street cleaner c. watchman d. All of them

B. Fill in the blanks.

1. A _________________ (farmer/gardener) grows food for us.
2. To keep our money safe, we put it in a ______________ (hospital/bank).
3. A ______________ (policeman/shopkeeper) sells things in a shop.
4. A ______________ (carpenter/dentist) makes furniture for us.

C. Write T for True and F for False.

1. A teacher teaches us in the classroom. ◯
2. A farmer stitches clothes for us. ◯
3. A postman delivers our letters and parcels. ◯
4. A fireman treats us when we fall sick. ◯

Subjective Type Questions

A. Choose the odd one out. Give reasons for the choice.

1. Classroom	Library	Post office	Playground
2. Bank	Hospital	Park	Factory
3. Eraser	Stamp	Envelope	Parcel
4. Dentist	Barber	Nurse	Doctor
5. Snowman	Policeman	Fireman	Watchman

B. Answer the following questions.

1. What does a farmer do for us?

____

____

2. How does a carpenter help us?

____

____

3. You see a thief entering your neighbour's house. Who will you call?

____

____

4. Where do children play in the evening?

____

____

5. Who will you call if there is a fire accident?

____

____

Application-based Question

Anusha's mother wants to buy some vegetables to make a curry. Where should she go to buy vegetables?

Picture-based Questions

A. Look at the picture and answer the following questions.

1. Identify and name this place.
2. When do we visit this place?
3. Name two people who work here.
4. Do you have this place in your neighbourhood?

B. Match the following people with their tools.

1. Shopkeeper 2. Doctor 3. Barber 4. Carpenter

a. 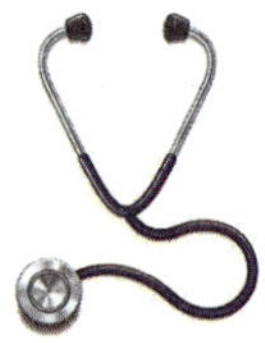

b. 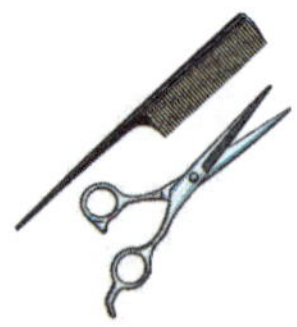

c. 

d. 

Skill Booster

A. **21CS:** Critical Thinking, Life Skills | **BT:** Cognitive

Identify and write the telephone numbers of the following important places.

B. **21CS:** Critical Thinking, Life Skills | **EL** | **BT:** Affective, Psychomotor

Keep your neighbourhood clean!

- Do not throw garbage on the road.
- Use a dustbin in the park, on the roadside and in the market.
- Grow more plants and do not pluck flowers.

Write two more ways to keep your neighbourhood clean. Make a poster on "Keep Your Neighbourhood Clean".

C. **21CS:** Collaboration, Life Skills | **BT:** Cognitive, Affective

Your bus broke down on your way to school. Your friend, Amit, was angry as he was getting late for the class assembly. He yelled at the bus driver. What should you do? Tick (✔) the correct option.

☐ Join Amit and scold the bus driver.

☐ Keep quiet and tell your teacher later.

☐ Tell Amit not to be rude and talk politely.

Worksheet 9

My SEE Journal

A. Do you like to go to school? Why or why not?

____

____

____

____

____

B. Name one activity that you do at school with your friends.

My SDG Journal

11 SUSTAINABLE CITIES AND COMMUNITIES

A. Why do you think every child should go to school?

____

____

____

____

____

B. Suppose you know a child who makes very good drawings, but does not have crayons. How will you help him?

____

____

____

____

____

10 Plants

Prior Knowledge

- Small and big plants
- Names of some common plants

Learning Objectives

- Types of plants
- Parts of a plant
- Uses of plants
- Taking care of plants

LET'S GET STARTED

Go for a nature walk in the school garden with your teacher. Look at the different types of plants. Talk about the colour of leaves and shape and size of the trees. Draw the plant you like the most in the space given below.

Plants are all around us. Plants are found in forests, near our homes, schools and along the roads. They make our surroundings green. Let us learn about the different types of plants.

TYPES OF PLANTS

You must have seen plants in different shapes and sizes. You must have also seen plants on land as well as in waterbodies (such as lakes and ponds). Let us learn about different types of plants.

Big Plants

Some plants are big and strong. These are called **trees**. Trees have strong and wide wooden stems called **trunks**. Trees live for many years. Mango tree, banyan tree, coconut tree, pine tree and apple tree are some examples of trees. Different trees have different shapes and sizes.

Banyan tree

DO YOU KNOW?
The national tree of India is the banyan tree.

Small Plants

Some plants are not big and strong like trees. They are called **small plants**. Based on the type of their stems, small plants can be grouped as shrubs, herbs, climbers and creepers.

Shrubs

Some plants are small but strong and bushy. Those plants are called **shrubs**. Shrubs have thin and hard stems. Rose, *Hibiscus* and jasmine are some examples of shrubs.

Herbs

Very small plants having soft stems are called **herbs**. Brinjal, grass and tomato are some examples of herbs.

Climbers

Some plants have very weak stems so they cannot grow straight. They need support. These plants are called **climbers**. Bitter gourd, grapevine and money plant are some examples of climbers.

Creepers

Some plants with weak stems grow along the ground. These plants are called **creepers**. Strawberry, pumpkin and watermelon are some examples of creepers.

Rose plant: A shrub

Grass: A herb

Money plant: A climber

Pumpkin: A creeper

PARTS OF A PLANT

A plant has many parts. Each part performs a special role in the growth of a plant. Look at the following picture and read about the different parts of a plant.

Parts of a plant

WHAT DOES A PLANT NEED TO GROW?

A plant needs the following things to grow.

- Soil
- Water
- Sunlight
- Air

Things that a plant needs

QUICK REVISION

Fill in the blanks.

1. ______________ are big and strong.
2. A pumpkin is a ______________.
3. A rose plant is a ______________ plant.

Plants that Grow on Land

Some plants grow on land. These are called **terrestrial plants**. Ashoka tree, palm tree, *Hibiscus* and banana are some plants that grow on land.

Palm tree

Plants that Grow in Water

Some plants grow in water. These are called **aquatic plants**. Lotus, lily and water hyacinth are some examples of aquatic plants.

Lily plant

DO YOU KNOW?

The national flower of India is lotus.

Plants That Give Us Medicines

Many medicines are made from plants such as *tulsi*, cloves, neem, mint and *Aloe vera*.

Mint leaves

Cloves

USES OF PLANTS

Plants not only make our surroundings beautiful but they are also useful to us. Most of the food we eat comes from plants. Plants give us fruits and vegetables. Some of the plant parts that we eat are given here.

Plant part	Examples
Leaves	Cabbage, spinach and coriander
Roots	Radish, turnip and carrot
Stems	Potato, ginger and sugarcane
Flowers	Cauliflower, broccoli and banana flower
Seeds	Cereals and pulses
Fruits	Guava, mango, banana and orange

TAKING CARE OF PLANTS

Plants make our surroundings green. They also give us oxygen. So, we should take care of plants. We should water them regularly. We should not cut trees.

DO YOU KNOW?

The national fruit of India is mango.

Girl watering plants

CONCEPT MAP

Plants

Plants need air, water, sunlight and soil to grow.

Types of plants

Big plants: Mango tree

Shrubs: Rose plant

Herbs: Brinjal

Climbers: Money plant

Creepers: Pumpkin

Where do plants grow?

On land and in water

Parts of plants that we eat

- **Leaves:** Spinach
- **Roots:** Carrot
- **Stems:** Potato
- **Flowers:** Cauliflower
- **Seeds:** Rice

KEYWORDS

Trees: big and strong plants

Herbs: small plants with soft stems

Shrubs: bushy plants with thin and hard stems

Climbers: plants that need support to grow straight

Creepers: plants that grow along the ground

Medicinal plants: plants that give us medicines

Exercise

Objective Type Questions

A. Choose the correct answer.

1. A plant that needs support to grow straight is called a ____________.
   a. tree b. climber c. bush d. grass
2. ____________ is a small plant.
   a. A neem tree b. *Hibiscus* c. A palm tree d. A mango tree
3. ____________ is a seed that we eat.
   a. Guava b. Turnip c. Mint d. Wheat
4. We eat the stem of ____________.
   a. potato b carrot c. rice d. orange
5. Plants do not need ____________ to grow.
   a. air b. water c. toys d. sunlight

B. Name the following.

1. A tree ____________________
2. A fruit that we eat ____________________
3. A vegetable that we eat ____________________
4. Seeds that we eat ____________________

C. Fill in the blanks.

1. Trees are ____________ (small/big) and ____________ (strong/weak) plants.
2. ____________ (Carrot/Sugarcane) is a root that we eat.
3. ____________ (Lotus/Money plant) is a plant that needs support to grow.
4. We should not ____________ (care for/cut) trees.

Subjective Type Questions

A. Define the following.

1. Trees
2. Herbs
3. Shrubs
4. Climbers
5. Creepers

B. Answer the following questions.

1. Where do you find plants growing?

____

____

2. What does a plant need to grow?

____

____

3. Name some plants from which we get medicines.

____

____

4. How can we take care of plants?

____

____

5. Why should we not cut trees?

____

____

Application-based Question

Money plant needs support of a stick to grow tall and straight. Why?

Picture-based Question

Look at the pictures given below. Cross (✗) the wrong actions and tick (✓) the right action.

1. 

Watering plants

2. 

Caring for plants

3. 

Cutting down trees

Skill Booster

A. **21CS:** Creativity and Innovation | AI | IF | **BT:** Psychomotor

Draw and colour the national fruit and the national flower of India.

B. **21CS:** Critical Thinking, Life Skills | **CC:** English | **BT:** Cognitive, Affective

One day, Tweety, the little blue bird returned to the jungle to find that her home was gone. The tall tree that nested her home was cut down by a woodcutter. Who else do you think lost its home? Tick (✓) the correct option.

☐ The tiger

☐ The jellyfish

☐ The woodpecker

What can be done so that animals do not lose their homes? Write two ways.

Worksheet 10

My SEE Journal

A. What kind of a girl is Alisha? Describe in a word or a sentence.

B. Which is your favourite pet animal? Why?

My SDG Journal

13 CLIMATE ACTION

A. Name a plant that you would like to grow and why. With your parents, visit a nearby nursery and buy that plant. Plant it in your school or park and take care of it.

B. Why do you think planting trees is important for our environment?

11 Animals

Prior Knowledge

- Names of some animals
- Names of some birds

Learning Objectives

- Big and small animals
- Where do animals live?
- Wild animals
- Domestic animals
- Birds
- Sounds of some animals and birds

LET'S GET STARTED

Connect the numbers to find the animal. Also, write its name.

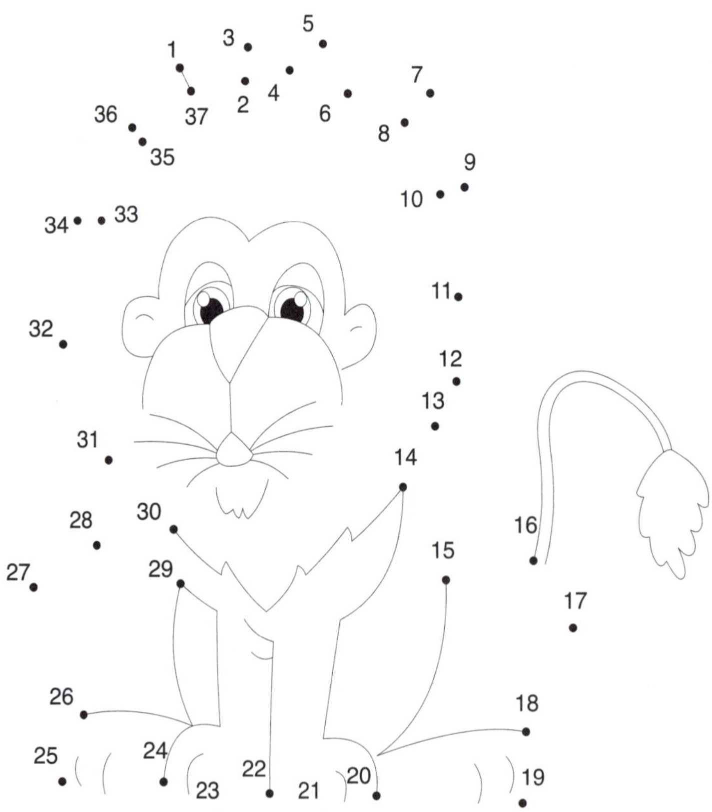

L ___ O ___

BIG AND SMALL ANIMALS

There are animals of different sizes in the world.

- Some animals are big such as the rhinoceros, elephant and giraffe.

Rhinoceros

Giraffe

- Some animals are small such as mouse, squirrel and rabbit.

Mouse

Squirrel

WHERE DO ANIMALS LIVE?

- Most animals live on land such as deer, lion, giraffe, zebra and elephant.

Deer

Lion

- Some animals live in water, such as fish, turtle and dolphin.

Fish

Turtle

- Some animals live on trees such as monkeys, koalas and squirrels.

Monkey

Koala

- Some animals live both on land and in water, such as frog and salamander.

Frog

Salamander

QUICK REVISION

Fill in the blanks.

1. Elephant is a ________ (big/small) animal.
2. A ________ (turtle/deer) lives in water.
3. Monkeys live ________ (on trees/in water).
4. A ________ (mouse/zebra) is a small animal.

DO YOU KNOW?

Blue whale is the largest animal in the world.

WILD ANIMALS

Animals that live in forests are called **wild animals** such as lion, tiger and bear.

Tiger

Lion

Bear

DOMESTIC ANIMALS

Animals that are kept on farms or in our houses are called **domestic animals**.

Farm Animals

We keep some domestic animals on the farm. They are called **farm animals**. Cow, hen and horse are some examples of farm animals.

Cow

Hen

Farm animals are given good food and kept in special homes.

A ***shed*** *for cows*

A ***coop*** *for hens*

A ***stable*** *for horses*

Farm animals are useful to us in many ways. Cows give us milk. Oxen help us **plough** the land. Goats give us milk and meat. Horses and donkeys help us in carrying loads. Hens and ducks give us eggs and meat.

> **WORD TO KNOW**
> plough: to turn soil over to loosen it

Pet Animals

We keep some domestic animals at home. They are called **pet animals**.

We feed them and take care of them. We also play with them. When they are sick, we take them to an animal doctor. A doctor who treats sick animals is called a **vet**. Pets are useful to us. A dog guards our house. A cat keeps our house free of mice.

Dog, cat and rabbit are some common animals that we keep as pets. Some people also keep fish in aquariums.

Dog

Cat

Rabbit

Fish

Some pet animals

BIRDS

We see many birds around us. Birds have wings and feathers. Wings help them fly. Some birds that can fly in the air are crow, sparrow and pigeon.

Crow Sparrow Pigeon

Some birds that can fly

Some birds such as emu, penguin and ostrich can only run and walk on land. They cannot fly.

Emu Penguin Ostrich

Some birds that cannot fly

Some birds such as duck, swan and pelican can swim in water.

Duck Swan Pelican

Some birds that can swim in water

TALK TIME

Why the birds such as emu, penguin and ostrich cannot fly?

SOUNDS OF SOME ANIMALS AND BIRDS

Animals and birds make different types of sounds. Some examples of sounds made by a few animals and birds are given below.

Duck *Sparrow* *Dog* *Cat* *Cow*

DO IT YOURSELF

Find out the sounds made by the following animals and birds.

1. Lion ______________ 2. Monkey ______________
3. Parrot ______________ 4. Owl ______________
5. Squirrel ______________ 6. Goat ______________

CONCEPT MAP

Where do animals live?

On land: Deer, Tiger

On trees: Monkey, Squirrel

In water: Fish, Dolphin

Both on land and in water: Frog, Crocodile

Big animals: Elephant, Giraffe

Small animals: Mouse, Rabbit

Animals → can be → Wild / Domestic

- Wild → live in → Forests → examples → Lion, Bear
- Domestic → live on → Farms → examples → Cow, Hen

Birds

↓

Birds have wings and feathers

↓

Birds that can fly in air: Crow, Sparrow

↓

Birds that cannot fly: Emu, Ostrich

↓

Birds that swim in water: Duck, Swan

KEYWORDS

Wild animals: animals that live in forests

Domestic animals: animals that live in our house or on farms

Farm animals: animals that live on a farm

Pet animals: animals that live in our house

Vet: the doctor who treats sick animals

Exercise

Objective Type Questions

A. Choose the correct answer.

1. ____________ animals live in a forest.

   a. Wild   b. Pet   c. Farm   d. Domestic

2. A ____________ lives both on land and in water.

   a. fish   b. salamander   c. whale   d. dolphin

3. We build a ____________ to keep horses.

   a. stable   b. kennel   c. coop   d. shed

4. ____________ gives us milk.

   a. An ox   b. A goat   c. A horse   d. A donkey

5. ____________ is a flightless bird.

   a. Emu   b. Pigeon   c. Crow   d. Sparrow

B. Fill in the blanks.

1. A ____________ (camel/frog) lives both on land and in water.
2. A cow is kept in a ____________ (coop/shed).
3. When our pets fall sick, we take them to a ____________ (farmer/vet).
4. A dog ____________ (guards/breaks) our house.
5. Birds have ____________ (hands/feathers) and ____________ (wings/teeth).

C. Write T for True and F for False.

1. Animals that live in forests are called domestic animals. ◯
2. All birds have wings. ◯
3. A rabbit is a small animal. ◯
4. A goat gives us milk and meat. ◯

D. Arrange the words in proper sequence.

1. is / mouse / small / a / animal
2. monkeys / on / live / trees
3. a / is / domestic / cow / animal

Subjective Type Questions

A. Differentiate between the following.

1. Wild animals and domestic animals
2. Farm animals and pet animals

B. Answer the following questions.

1. What are pet animals?

____

2. Name two big animals.

____

3. How does a cow help us?

____

4. What should we do if our pet is sick?

____

Application-based Question

We give food to our pets. Where do wild animals get their food from?

Picture-based Question

Write W for wild and D for domestic animals.

1. 

Dog

2. 

Tiger

3. 

Goat

4. 

Crocodile

Skill Booster

A. 21CS: Creativity and Innovation, Information Literacy | AI | BT: Cognitive, Psychomotor

Collect pictures of the various animals and their homes and paste them in your scrapbook. Decorate the spread by doing some artwork. Show your scrapbook to your teacher.

B. 21CS: Life Skills | BT: Affective

Care for Our Feathered Friends

It is very hot during summers and sometimes birds do not get enough water. Keep a bowl of water outside on the windowsill for birds to come and drink water from. This is one way to care for our feathered friends. What else can you do for them?

Worksheet 11

Bhavya is a five-year-old girl. She studies in Class 1. She has a pet dog. Its name is Cooper. She takes care of Cooper and plays with it. Cooper also loves playing with Bhavya.

My SEE Journal

Draw or paste a picture of yourself with your pet.

My SDG Journal

A. Why do we keep some animals as pets?

____

____

____

____

____

B. How do you feel when you see animals locked up in cages or in zoos?

____

____

____

____

____

____

12 Transport

Prior Knowledge

- Some of the reasons for travelling from one place to another: children go to school, parents go to office, visiting relatives, going on vacation
- Names of some vehicles: cars, scooters, aeroplanes and trains

Learning Objectives

- Transport
- Parts of vehicles
- Traffic police and traffic light
- Emergency vehicles
- Avoiding misuse of transport

LET'S GET STARTED

1. Bus
2. Motorcycle
3. Car
4. Helicopter

a. 

b. 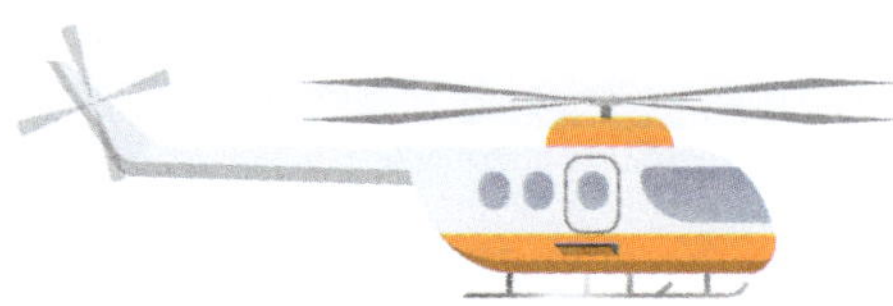

c. 

d. 

How did you come to school today? ____________________

TRANSPORT

We go from one place to another. This is called **travelling**. We travel to different places based on our needs. For example, children go to school and adults go to their colleges or offices to work.
To travel from one place to another, we need means of transport.

> **WORD TO KNOW**
> transport: something that carries people or things from one place to another such as a car, scooter and bus

To go to your friend's house in the same city, you may travel by a car or bus. But to go to your friend's house in another city, you may have to travel by train or an aeroplane.

There are three modes of transport.

- Land transport
- Air transport
- Water transport

Land Transport

The means of transport that move on land are called **land transport**. Land transport can be of two types: road transport and rail transport.

Some means of road transport are truck, cycle and bus.

Some means of road transport

Some means of road transport move very fast, while others move very slowly.

Trains are a means of rail transport. They move on railway tracks. They carry many people and goods over long distances.

See the table below with means of land transport grouped on the basis of the number of wheels each one has.

Train

Two wheels	Three wheels	Four wheels	More than four wheels
bicycle	tricycle	car	train
bullock cart	autorickshaw	jeep	metro
motorcycle	rickshaw	van	truck
scooter			

Air Transport

The means of transport that travel in the air are called **air transport**. Some means of air transport are aeroplane and helicopter. Aeroplanes travel at very high speeds. They carry people and goods over a long distance in a short time.

Aeroplane

DO YOU KNOW?

People travelling to space use a special means of transport called a space shuttle.

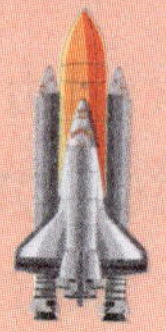

Water Transport

The means of transport that sail over water are called **water transport**. These means of water transport help us travel across rivers and oceans. Some means of water transport are ship, boat and yacht. Ships can carry many people and goods at the same time.

Ship

PARTS OF VEHICLES

Do you know the names of different parts of the following vehicles?

Parts of a Car

Look at the picture given below to know the different parts of a car.

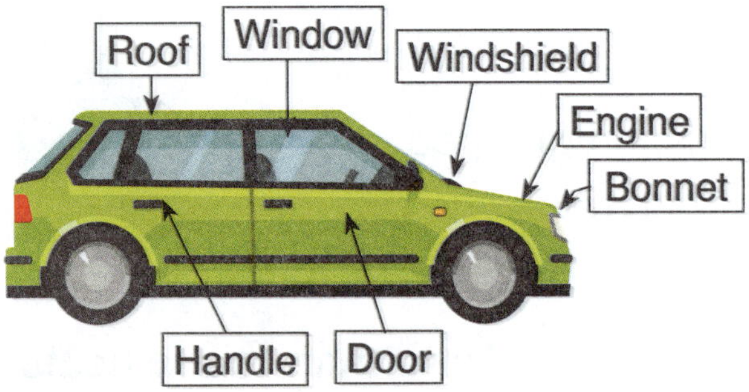

Parts of an Aeroplane

Look at the picture given below to read and learn the names of the different parts of an aeroplane.

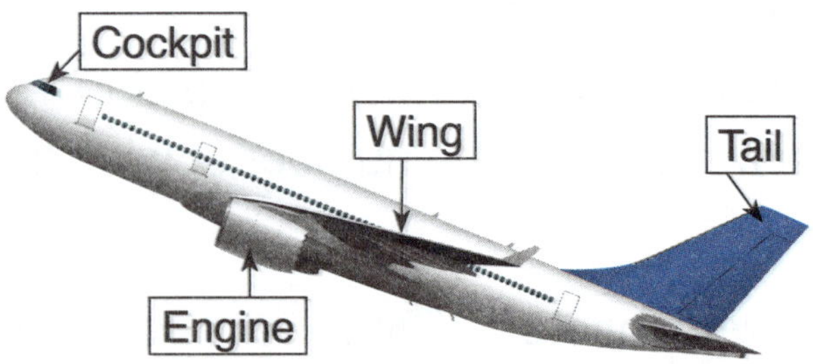

DO IT YOURSELF

Draw or paste pictures of a train and a sailboat in your scrapbook and label their parts.

We should be thankful to all the people who help us travel by different means of transport. Refer to the below table to learn about some of the people who help us travel by different means of transport.

Vehicle	People who help
Bus	Driver, conductor and ticket collector
Car	Driver and mechanic
Aeroplane	Pilot, air hostess, cabin crew and ground crew
Ship	Captain, crew and sailors
Train	Engine driver, ticket collector, guard and service men

QUICK REVISION

Write T for True and F for False.

1. We can cross an ocean in a ship. ◯
2. A cycle needs petrol to run. ◯
3. A train moves on railway tracks. ◯
4. A bus is a means of water transport. ◯

Noise in the Surroundings by Vehicles

Transport also adds to the noise, especially in crowded places such as cities. What causes noise in the surroundings?

- Horns of vehicles running on the road
- Aeroplanes taking off and landing

Do not blow horns near schools and hospitals.

Remember, loud noise can make us deaf.

Vehicles honking

TRAFFIC POLICE AND TRAFFIC LIGHT

We should always travel safe. To keep ourselves safe, we need to follow traffic rules.

A traffic policeman controls traffic to make sure the vehicles move smoothly on the road. He fines people who do not obey traffic rules.

Traffic policeman

Have you noticed a traffic light while travelling to school?
A **traffic light** at the traffic signal controls traffic.

Cross the road only when the **pedestrian** lights are green. Always hold your parent's or an elder's hand while crossing the road.

Children crossing the road when the pedestrian light is green

A boy crossing the road holding an elder's hand

A POEM!

What Does a Traffic Light Say?

Traffic light, traffic light,
why do you blink?

To help us cross, that's
what I think!

'Stop' says the red light,
green says 'go'.

'Wait' says the yellow light,
I am sure you know!

EMERGENCY VEHICLES

Here are some vehicles that we use in case of an emergency.

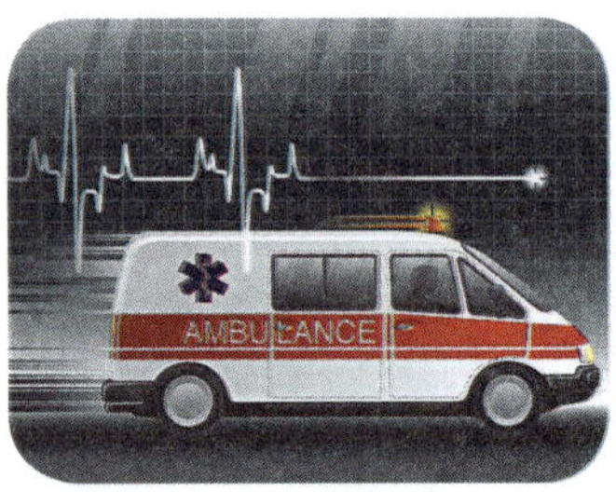

An **ambulance** *carries sick people to the hospital.*

A **police van** *helps police reach quickly.*

A **fire engine** *carries firemen and a tank of water to put out a fire.*

AVOIDING MISUSE OF TRANSPORT

- We must save **fuel** by walking or riding a bicycle to travel short distances.
- While travelling in a bus or train, we must not damage or dirty it.
- We must not ask the driver to race on the road.

A boy riding a bicycle

WORD TO KNOW

pedestrian: people who walk on the road

fuel: petrol, diesel

CONCEPT MAP

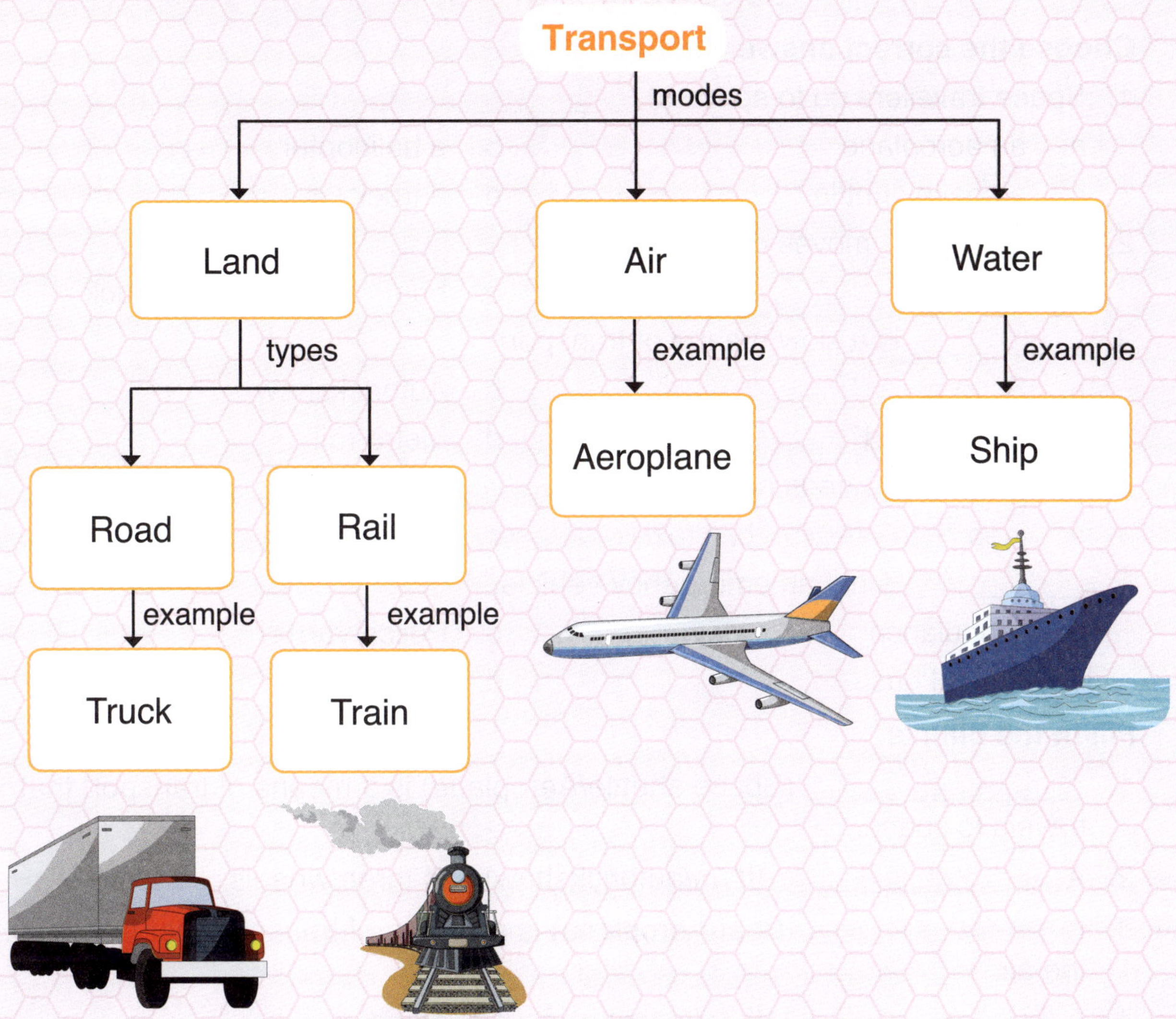

KEYWORDS

Transport: to move things and people from one place to another

Land transport: means of transport that move on land

Water transport: means of transport that move over water

Air transport: means of transport that move in the air

Exercise

Objective Type Questions

A. Choose the correct answer.

1. Space travellers go to space in __________.
   a. an aeroplane b. a helicopter
   c. a space shuttle d. a truck
2. A __________ moves on tracks.
   a. train b. car c. bus d. truck
3. __________ is a slow means of transport.
   a. Scooter b. Autorickshaw
   c. Bullock cart d. Metro rail
4. A __________ needs no fuel to move.
   a. jeep b. taxi c. bicycle d. van
5. __________ is not an emergency vehicle.
   a. Ambulance b. Police van
   c. School bus d. Fire engine

B. Fill in the blanks.

1. ________________ (Space shuttle/Aeroplane) is a means of transport that travels to space.
2. A ________________ (train/autorickshaw) has three wheels.
3. ________________ (Boat/Aeroplane) is a means of transport that flies in the air.
4. A ________________ (boat/scooter) sails over water.
5. A ________________ (train/car) moves on road.

Subjective Type Questions

A. Define the following.

1. Transport
2. Land transport
3. Water transport
4. Air transport

B. Answer the following questions.

1. Why do we need transport?

   ____

2. What are the two types of land transport?

   ____

3. Name any three means of water transport.

4. Draw an aeroplane and label its main parts.

Application-based Question

One day, Anaisha's father was driving her to school. In his car's rear view mirror, he saw an ambulance behind them. He moved his car to the side and made way for the ambulance. Why do you think Anaisha's father did that?

Picture-based Question

Look at the picture and answer the following questions.

1. What is shown in this picture?
2. Have you seen it before? If yes, where?
3. Colour it and write the meaning of each colour.

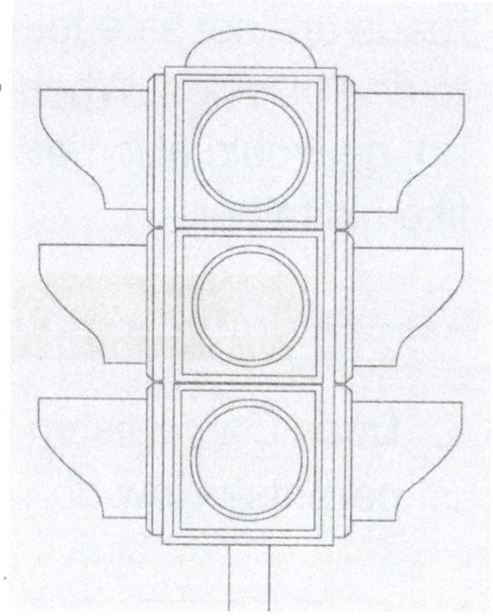

Skill Booster

A. **21CS:** Information Literacy | **BT:** Psychomotor

Collect six pictures of different means of transport. Paste them in your scrapbook and name them.

B. **21CS:** Critical Thinking, Life Skills | **BT:** Cognitive, Affective

If you are going to a place nearby, you should either walk or ride your cycle. Write two advantages of riding a bicycle.

Worksheet 12

This is Daniel and his father. Today, they went to the market on a bicycle to buy some groceries. They always walk down or use a bicycle to go to the nearby places.

Daniel can also ride a bicycle, but he rides only in the compound and not on the road. His father says that roads are not safe for small children to ride bicycles. When Daniel grows up, he would also ride on the road like his father.

My SEE Journal

A. Does Daniel listen to his parents? How do you know this?

B. What should you do to show that you listen to your parents?

My SDG Journal

4 QUALITY EDUCATION

A. Why do Daniel and his father walk down or use a bicycle to go to the nearby places?

B. Why should small children not ride bicycles on the roads?

13 Communication

Prior Knowledge

- Names of some common means of communication: mobile phone, letter and newspaper

Learning Objectives

- Communication
- Means of communication
- Computers

LET'S GET STARTED

Name the following pictures shown below.

1. 

   ____

2. 

   ____

3. 

   ____

4. 

   ____

COMMUNICATION

Communication means sharing of information, ideas and news.

We would not know about each other's ideas and about what is happening in other places or around the world if we do not communicate.

We mainly communicate using our voice.

DO YOU KNOW?

We can also communicate through dance, songs and drawings.

MEANS OF COMMUNICATION

The best way to communicate is by simply talking to each other. But sometimes, it is not possible to talk to each other. So we use different ways to communicate.

Some means through which we share information with each other are as follows.

Children talking to each other

Letter

Telephone

Radio

Newspaper

Mobile phone

Television

Magazines

Books

Some means of communication

We can send letters to people by post. Talking over the phone helps you communicate with someone quickly. You may talk to people in other cities or even in different countries on the telephone.

FIND OUT

Find out the names of two newspapers and two magazines.

We can carry a mobile phone with us wherever we go. We use it to talk to people and send text messages or **SMS**. Smart phones also allow us to watch the person while we speak to him or her.

WORD TO KNOW

SMS: short message service; it is a way of sending short messages from one mobile phone to another

QUICK REVISION

Fill in the blanks.

1. ____________ means sharing of ideas and news.
2. We mainly communicate using our ____________.
3. We can watch the person while we speak to him/her through ____________.

COMPUTERS

All of you must have seen or used a computer or laptop.

Computer

Laptop

We can send electronic mails or e-mails using a computer when it is connected to the Internet.

DO YOU KNOW?

Computers help us in many ways in our daily lives. We book tickets for travel on computers. Traffic lights are controlled by computers. We pay bills in malls through computers. We also use smart boards in our classrooms to gather information and to learn. This is called using information and communications technology (ICT).

CONCEPT MAP

KEYWORDS

Communication: sharing ideas and information

Means of communication: different ways to communicate with each other

Exercise

Objective Type Questions

A. Choose the correct answer.

1. We post our letters in a __________.
   - a. post box b. ATM
   - c. milk booth d. None of these
2. Which means of communication will you use to wish your friends on their birthdays?
   - a. Newspaper b. Mobile phone
   - c. Radio d. Television
3. We cannot send e-mails using a __________.
   - a. computer b. laptop
   - c. mobile phones d. radio
4. We can share information with many people using a __________.
   - a. postcard b. letter
   - c. newspaper d. telephone
5. __________ is not a means of communication.
   - a. Internet b. Telephone
   - c. Letter d. Magazine

B. Arrange the words in proper sequence.

1. communication / of / means / ideas / sharing
2. mainly /our /communicate / we / using / voice
3. by / can / to / send / we / people / letters / post
4. we / send / can / a / e-mails / computer / using

C. What will you use?

1. To talk to your friend who lives in another city __________
2. To send a message to your grandmother immediately __________
3. To watch a cricket match happening in England __________

Subjective Type Questions

A. Choose the odd one out. Give reasons for the choice.

1. Books	Magazines	Newspaper	Telephone
2. Television	Newspaper	Radio	Mobile phone
3. Laptop	Computer	Smart phone	Telephone
4. Land phone	Mobile phone	Books	Television
5. Camera	Television	Mobile phone	Computer

B. Answer the following questions.

1. What is communication?

   ____

2. Name two ways in which you can communicate with a person living in the same city.

   ____

3. What is the quickest way of sending e-mail to a person in another city?

   ____

Application-based Question

Rani wants a glass of water. But she cannot speak due to a bad throat infection. How will she communicate her need to a friend?

Picture-based Question

Match the following.

1. 

2. 

3. 

a. News b. E-mail c. SMS

Skill Booster

A. 21CS: Creativity and Innovation | BT: Psychomotor

Make Your Own Telephone!

You will need: Ice cream cups and a thick string

Let us start: Ask an adult to make a hole at the base of each cup. Take a thick string and put the cups at the two ends of the string. Your telephone is ready. Now talk to your friend through the cup.

B. 21CS: Life Skills | EL | BT: Affective

With an elder go to the nearby post office and buy a post card. Write a letter to your parents thanking them for everything they do for you. Write your complete address in the address box. Post it in the post box. Wait till it reaches your address. Write how did your parents feel upon reading your letter?

Worksheet 13

Nimesh is on a video call with his grandmother.

My SEE Journal

A. What do you do when you miss somebody?

____

____

____

____

____

B. Who do you call most of the times and why?

____

____

____

____

____

My SDG Journal

9 INDUSTRY, INNOVATION AND INFRASTRUCTURE

A. Write two uses of the Internet.

____

____

____

____

____

B. What are the other means of communication? Write any three.

____

____

____

____

____

14 The World Around Me: Sun, Moon, Sky and Stars

Prior Knowledge

- Sun appears in the day sky
- Moon and stars appear at night
- Three seasons: hot, rainy and cold

Learning Objectives

- Sky in the daytime
- Sky at night: stars, moon
- Weather and seasons

LET'S GET STARTED

The sky looks different at different times of the day. In the morning, we see the sun and the clouds. At night, we see the moon, stars and clouds.

Look at the pictures given below. Which one shows day and which one shows night? Write in the space given below each picture.

1

This is ________.

2

This is ________.

THE SUN

Sun

The sun shines brightly during the day. It is a big ball of fire in the sky. The sun gives us heat and light. The sun rises in the morning and sets in the evening. A new day begins when the sun rises. It becomes night when the sun sets. The sun rises in the east and sets in the west.

A POEM!

What do we see when we look at the sky?
Clouds float across, up so high.
The sun shines bright, giving us light.
The moon does the same when it's night.
After the rain, we see a rainbow.
Flashing across the sky, making it glow.
The stars are there to shine and twinkle.
Making our world smile and sparkle!

THE MOON

The moon shines in the sky at night. It looks like a white ball in the sky. The moon changes its shape every night. Sometimes, we see the full moon; sometimes a part of it and sometimes no moon at all. We cannot see the moon in the daytime because of the bright light of the sun. The moon has no light of its own. It shines due to the light of the sun that falls on it.

Shapes of the moon

The shape of the moon actually does not change. As the moon moves around the Earth, we see only that part of the moon that is lighted by the sun's rays.

CLOUDS

We see white, fluffy clouds **floating** across the sky. On a rainy day, dark clouds cover the sky.

Sometimes after the rain, we see a rainbow in the sky! Violet, Indigo, Blue, Green, Yellow, Orange and Red (VIBGYOR) are the seven colours that you see in a rainbow.

Rainbow

WORD TO KNOW

float: to move around gently in the sky

STARS

Stars shine at night. They seem to twinkle in the night sky.

Stars are very big in size. They look very small because they are very far from us.

Stars

DO YOU KNOW?

The sun is also a star.

QUICK REVISION

Write T for True and F for False.

1. The sun is a big ball of fire in the sky. ◯
2. The moon looks like a yellow ball in the sky. ◯
3. On a rainy day, dark clouds cover the sky. ◯
4. Stars are very small in size. ◯

WEATHER AND SEASONS

The weather changes every day. Some days are sunny, some are cloudy, some are foggy, some are rainy, some are windy and some are very cold. When the weather remains the same for a long time, we call it a **season**. In India, we have three main seasons: summer, monsoon and winter.

Summer

Summer is the hottest season. The sun shines brightly and the days are very hot. During summer, we like to stay indoors near a fan or an air conditioner. We like to drink cold drinks and have ice creams in this season. During summer, we like to wear light clothes made of cotton. Cotton clothes keep our body cool.

Juby and John enjoying ice cream on a hot summer day

Monsoon

The rainy season is also called **monsoon**.

Before it rains, dark clouds cover the sky. Sometimes it rains very heavily, while sometimes, it only drizzles.

WORD TO KNOW
drizzle: very light rain

We carry an umbrella or wear a raincoat and gumboots when it rains. They protect us from the rain.

Children wearing raincoats, gumboots and carrying umbrellas

Winter

Winter is the coldest season. Days are very cold. Nights are colder and longer. During winter, we like to sit in front of a fire and enjoy its warmth. We wear woollen clothes such as sweaters to keep our body warm. We like to eat hot food and have hot drinks such as soup and hot milk.

In some places, it snows heavily during winter.

Umair and Rukhsar enjoying hot soup near the fireplace on a cold day

CONCEPT MAP

Sky

- **Sun:** Gives us heat and light
- **Moon:** Shines at night, changes shape every night
- **Clouds:** White and fluffy, float across the sky
- **Stars:** Shine at night

Weather and Seasons

- Weather changes everyday
- Season is when the weather remains the same for many days
  - **Summer:** Hot season
  - **Winter:** Cold season
  - **Monsoons:** Rainy season

KEYWORDS

Sun: brightly shining object in the day sky

Moon: white bright ball in the night sky

Stars: small twinkling lights seen in the night sky

Clouds: white fluffy shapes floating across the sky on a clear day

Weather: the conditions (such as hot, rainy, sunny and cold) in an area at a particular time

Season: the condition when weather remains the same for a long time

Exercise

Objective Type Questions

A. Choose the correct answer.

1. The sun is a ____________.
   a. planet b. star c. moon d. cloud
2. ____________ is the hottest season.
   a. Summer b. Winter c. Autumn d. Spring
3. We wear gumboots in ____________.
   a. summer b. winter c. monsoon d. autumn
4. We do not see ____________ in the day sky.
   a. clouds b. the sun c. stars d. a rainbow
5. We do not use ____________ in summer.
   a. air conditioners b. refrigerators c. room heaters d. fans

B. Write T for True and F for False.

1. Cotton clothes keep our body warm. ◯
2. During winter, nights are long. ◯
3. When the sun sets, night begins. ◯
4. Clouds are made of cotton. ◯
5. The sun is a star. ◯

C. Fill in the blanks.

1. In the morning, we see the __________ (sun/moon) and the __________ (clouds/stars).
2. The sun gives us _________ (wood/heat) and _________ (light/water).
3. Rainy season is also known as __________ (fall/monsoon).
4. The weather changes __________ (every day/every month).
5. The moon changes its __________ (place/shape) every night.

Subjective Type Questions

A. Give reasons for the following.

1. We cannot see the moon in the daytime.
2. We like to stay indoors near a fan or air conditioner in the summer season.
3. We wear woollen clothes in the winter season.

B. Answer the following questions.

1. What do we get from the sun?

   ____

   ____

2. Why can we not see the moon during the day?

____

3. Why do stars look small in the sky?

____

4. Why do we wear cotton clothes in summer season?

____

5. What is a season?

____

Application-based Question

It is a bright and sunny day. Seema's little brother Soham wants to go out and play. He asks Seema what he should wear. Seema tells him to wear a sweater and a muffler. Is Seema right? Why or why not?

Picture-based Question

Look at the pictures given below. When do you see them? Draw a table with two columns labelled as Day and Night. Draw the following items in the correct columns.

Skill Booster

A. 21CS: Creativity and Innovation | AI | BT: Affective, Psychomotor

Make a Night Sky!

Take white paper and a black crayon. Colour the white paper completely with the black crayon leaving no gap. Now, using the nib of a ballpoint pen (with no ink) or the pointed back of a paint brush, draw stars and moon on the paper. Your night sky is ready!

B. 21CS: Critical Thinking, Life Skills | BT: Cognitive

We get heat and light from the sun. If we can use sunlight to do our work, we can save electricity. For example, in the daytime, we use sunlight rather than tube lights or bulbs to see things around us.

Can you write another way in which we can use heat and light from the sun and save electricity?

Worksheet 14

Ravi is reading in sunlight.

Faiza is reading under a lampshade during daytime.

My SEE Journal

A. Who saves electricity: Ravi or Faiza? How?

____

____

____

____

____

B. Name all the activities that you do in sunlight.

____

____

____

____

____

My SDG Journal

12 RESPONSIBLE CONSUMPTION AND PRODUCTION

A. How does reading in sunlight save electricity?

____

____

____

____

B. How can you save electricity at school?

____

____

____

____

____

Review Corner

Review 1 (Chapters 1–3) **Maximum Marks: 25**

A. Label the body parts. **(5)**

B. Fill in the blanks. **(4)**

1. ____________________ are the activities we like to do in our free time.
2. ____________________ organs help us know the world around us.
3. My uncle's son is my ____________________.
4. We eat ____________________ to live, grow, stay healthy and strong.

C. Name the following. **(4)**

1. The meal taken in the morning ____________________
2. Those who eat food from plants only ____________________
3. The sense organ that helps us feel ____________________
4. Your mother's mother ____________________

D. Match the following. **(4)**

1. 
2. 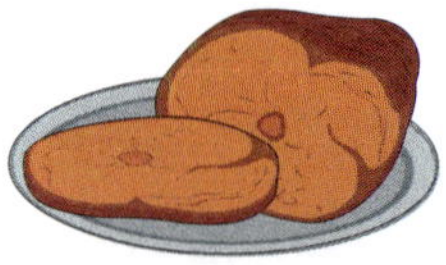
3. 
4. 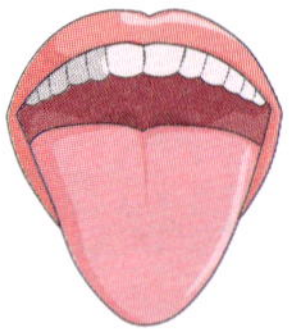

a. Healthy food

b. Taste

c. Cutlery

d. Needs to be cooked before eating

E. Answer the following questions. **(6)**

1. Name the five sense organs. How do they help us?
2. Name and describe the different types of families.
3. Why do we eat food?

F. Draw and colour your favourite fruit and write its name. **(2)**

Review 2 (Chapters 4–7) Maximum Marks: 25

A. Write the uses of air shown by the pictures below. (4)

1.  ____________

2.  ____________

3.  ____________

4.  ____________

B. Fill in the blanks. (6)

1. Plants clean the ____________.
2. People who stay near our house are our ____________.
3. We must always wear ____________ clothes.
4. We wear a ____________ to school.
5. We brush our teeth and take bath in the ____________.
6. Moving air is called ____________.

C. Write T for True and F for False. (4)

1. River is the main source of all the water on the Earth. ◯
2. A policeman wears a uniform. ◯
3. A fireman uses water to put out fire. ◯
4. Each room in a house has its own use. ◯

D. Answer the following questions. (6)

1. Name any two things that we can decorate our house with.
2. Write two ways in which we can keep the air clean.
3. Why do we need water?

E. Name the following. (3)

1. The room in which we cook our food ____________
2. We wear this on a rainy day ____________
3. We need this to fill tyres and balloons ____________

F. Draw and colour a picture of a thing that you must carry on a rainy day. (2)

Review 3 (Chapters 8–10) Maximum Marks: 25

A. What are they doing? **(4)**

1.  ____________
2.  ____________
3.  ____________
4.  ____________

B. Name the following. **(6)**

1. He grows food for us ____________
2. He delivers our letters and parcels ____________
3. He drives us to school every morning ____________
4. They are tall and strong plants ____________
5. These plants need support to grow ____________
6. Black and white stripes at some places on the road ____________

C. Fill in the blanks. **(5)**

1. A ____________ is where we keep our money safe.
2. We wash our ____________ before and after meals.
3. We should not play with ____________ things.
4. A ____________ is a narrow path on the side of the road for walking.
5. ____________ surroundings make us ill.

D. Answer the following questions. **(8)**

1. What does a plant need to grow?
2. Name any four places in your neighbourhood.
3. Write two ways to stay clean.
4. How do we send e-mails?

E. Draw and colour any one thing that helps you stay clean. **(2)**

Review 4 (Chapters 11–14) Maximum Marks: 25

A. Write W for wild animals and D for domestic animals. (4)

1. 
2. 
3. 
4. 

B. Fill in the blanks. (6)

1. ________________ animals live with us in our home.
2. Birds such as penguins and ostriches cannot ________________.
3. A bus is a means of ________________ transport.
4. The best way to communicate is by ________________ to each other.
5. The sun gives us ________________ and ________________.

C. Name the following. (5)

1. A big ball of fire in the sky ________________
2. A white round ball in the night sky ________________
3. Sharing of information, ideas and news ________________
4. A vehicle that carries firemen and a tank of water ________________
5. A doctor who treats sick animals ________________

D. Write T for True and F for False. (5)

1. There are animals of different sizes in the world. ◯
2. A salamander lives both on land and in water. ◯
3. We keep all domestic animals in the house. ◯
4. An aeroplane travels over water. ◯
5. Trains move on railway tracks. ◯

E. Answer the following questions. (3)

1. Name any two big animals.
2. What are the three modes of transport?
3. Why do we need to communicate with each other?

F. Draw a picture of a vehicle that you would want to travel by. (2)

My Environment, My Responsibility!

No Littering in Park

A. Would you like to play in a littered park or picnic near a pond dumped with garbage that smells very bad?

____

B. There are many people who throw garbage on roads, parks and near or in waterbodies such as lakes, rivers and ponds. This makes our surroundings look dirty. Have you ever seen people who collect garbage and keep these places clean? Who are they?

____

Yes, you are right. They are called **cleaners**. However, they alone cannot keep our surroundings clean. We should also practise good habits and throw garbage only in wastebins, and not litter public places.

C. Do you litter your classroom and playground? Where do you throw waste papers and pencil shavings?

____

D. With your friends, form a club called "The Children's Club" and organize an event to clean your nearby park. Ask your parents for help. Write the names of the members of your club in the space given below.

____

____

____

E. Make a colourful poster on 'No Littering in Park'.

My Eco Craft: A Twig Photo Frame

Things You Need: A cardboard frame, twigs, coloured paper, satin ribbon, paint brush, paint, glue gun, flower punch and a pair of scissors

Note: Do not use scissors yourself. Take the help of an elder while cutting.

Let's Start!

Visit a nearby park or garden and collect some dried twigs or small branches. Do not pluck fresh twigs from the plants in the park.

1.

Colour the cardboard frame.

2.

Fix the twigs on all sides of the cardboard frame.

3.

Punch in the flowers.

4.

Fix the flowers above the twigs.

5.

Make a bow from the ribbon and fix it to the top right corner of the frame.

6.

Your twig photo frame is ready! Insert your family photo and keep it on your table.

Make a Stone Bunny

With the help of an elder, make a stone bunny. Write down the things that you will need and the steps to make it. Draw or paste a picture of your stone bunny in the space provided.

Things You Need: ____________________

____

____

____

Let's Start: ____________________

____

____

____

____

____

____

____

____

____

____

____

____

____

____

____